40 Days

with

Wesley

A Daily
Devotional Journey

Rueben P. Job

Compiled and Edited by
Pamela C. Hawkins

Abingdon Press / Nashville

40 DAYS WITH WESLEY

This book is printed on elemental chlorine-free paper.
ISBN 978-1-5018-3601-5

Scripture quotations unless noted otherwise are from the Common English Bible. Copyright © 2011 by the Common English Bible. All rights reserved. Used by permission. www.CommonEnglishBible.com.

Scripture quotations noted NRSV are taken from New Revised Standard Version of the Bible, copyright 1989, Division of Christian Education of the National Council of the Churches of Christ in the United States of America. Used by permission. All rights reserved.

All Wesley Readings and quotations noted *Works* are taken *The Works of John Wesley*, Thomas Jackson edition. 14 vol. Third edition, 1831, reprinted by the Wesleyan-Methodist Book Room in London, England, in 1872. References will be noted by volume:page numer.

Quotations noted *WSR* are from Rueben P. Job's *A Wesleyan Spiritual Reader*. Copyright 1998 by Abingdon Press.

Quotations noted *TSR* are from Rueben P. Job's *Three Simple Rules: A Wesleyan Way of Living*. Copyright 2007 by Abingdon Press.

Quotations noted *TSQ* are from Rueben P. Job's *Three Simple Questions: Knowing the God of Love, Hope, and Purpose*. Copyright 2011 by Abingdon Press.

Quotations noted *GTR* are from Rueben P. Job's *A Guide to Retreat for All God's Shepherds*. Copyright 1994 by Abingdon Press.

Quotations noted *WYP* are from Rueben P. Job's *When You Pray: Daily Practices for Prayerful Living*. Copyright 2009 by Abingdon Press.

Quotations noted *Listen* are from Rueben P. Job's *Listen: Praying in a Noisy World*. Copyright 2013 by Abingdon Press.

Quotations noted *BPC* are from Rueben P. Job's *Becoming a Praying Congregation: Churchwide Leadership Tools*. Copyright 2009 by Abingdon Press.

Quotations noted *UMH* are from *The United Methodist Hymnal*. Copyright 1989 by The United Methodist Publishing House. Used by permission.

17 18 19 20 21 22 23 24 25 26 — 10 9 8 7 6 5 4 3 2 1
PRINTED IN THE PEOPLE'S REPUBLIC OF CHINA

Contents

Foreword

Rueben P. Job knew how to love God and live abundantly! Every now and then we encounter people who cause us to stand quiet in admiration and profound awe. Their manner is humble yet alert, they think creatively and deeply, and when we are with them a sweet sustaining grace pours over us. Instinctively we know they've walked on higher, holy ground, and through their example our eyes, ears, hearts, and minds open up toward God with vivid expectancy and hope.

They help us go deeper in knowing and loving God. We learn to let loose our imagination, uncover new confidence, and acquire courage, so we might delight God and work for mercy and justice to help heal our hurting world.

Rueben P. Job was plainspoken and held fast to elegantly simple convictions. God created and loves the world and each of us. Jesus' love saves us from sin, and through his life, death, and resurrection he shows us what matters most. The Spirit moves ahead, with and behind us, sowing the fertile ground of creation with the seeds of love, reverence, gratitude, a hunger for justice, and joyful service.

Rueben demonstrated in an amazing and convincing way through eighty-six years among us that we can trust God. We can choose to love God and grow in grace. That's not the work of a select few but available to all who regularly engage Scripture, prayer, silence, and opening their hearts to God. He knew these patterns of attentive prayer and reflection were intensely transforming because he saw how they miraculously changed him and many others.

Rueben lived with gusto and passion. He cared about politics and science and art, and he was head-over-heels in love with the wonders of the outdoors. But when his body could no longer keep up with his dancing spirit and inventive mind, this seasoned farmer, pastor, Air Force chaplain, spiritual guide, prolific writer and bishop, loving husband, father, and friend approached death with the utter innocent confidence of a sleeping baby in a mother's arms.

Rueben is still teaching all of us how to love God and live abundantly.

—Neil M. Alexander

Introduction

Every now and then we see splendid examples of what it means to follow God as made known in Jesus. These persons, both young and old, live out the gospel in such clear ways that their lives can be explained only by God's dwelling within them. "How like Jesus! How like God!" we may exclaim as we observe their lives of compassion, love, and grace. As we see them living as Jesus taught us to live, in our hearts we whisper, "I want to be like that; I want to live like that; I want to belong to God like that." And we can love like that; we can live like that.

Through spiritual reading we can become connected to the saints who have gone before us. They can become for us companions on our journey and we can learn from them, be guided and directed by their experience and witness. Their voices can address our lives with insight and wisdom gained by faithful living and tested by centuries.

> O begin! Fix some part of every day for private exercises. You may acquire the taste for which you have not: What is tedious at first will afterwards be pleasant. Whether you like it or no, read and pray daily. It is for your life: there is no other way... Do justice to your own soul: give it time and means to grow.
>
> *"Letter to John Trembath,"* Works *12:254*
>
> *–Rueben Job*

Daily Pattern

- Prayer of Presence

- Scripture

- First Wesley Reading

- Reflections

- Second Wesley Reading

- Time for Silent Reflection
  and Journaling

- Blessing

The True God

Prayer of Presence

Creator God, author of all that is and lover of all that you have made, deepen our awareness of your mighty acts past and present and your constant presence with us every moment of our existence. Invade our minds, senses, and hearts like a quiet sunrise, a refreshing rain, a beautiful bouquet, a commanding voice, a trusted companion, and a loving touch—because we want to know you and remember who you are with every breath we take.

By the power of your grace, transform us more and more until we become beautiful reflections of your presence and likeness in all that we do and are, as we offer all that we are and have to you in the name and spirit of Christ. **Amen.**

Scripture

What you worship as unknown, I now proclaim to you. God, who made the world and everything in it, is Lord of heaven and earth. He doesn't live in temples made with human hands. Nor is God served by human hands, as though he needed something, since he is the one who gives life, breath, and everything else. From one person God created every human nation to live on the whole earth, having determined *their appointed times and the boundaries of their lands.... In fact, God isn't far away from any of us. In God we live, move, and exist. As some of your own poets said, "We are his offspring."*

Acts 17:23b-28

First Wesley Reading

And as the true God, he is also the Supporter of all the things that he hath made. He beareth, upholdeth, sustaineth, all created things by the word of his power, by the same powerful word which brought them out of nothing. As this was absolutely necessary for the beginning of their existence, it is equally so for the continuance of it: Were his almighty influence withdrawn, they could not subsist a moment longer. Hold up a stone in the air; the moment you withdraw your hand, it naturally falls to the ground. In like manner, were he to withdraw his hand for a moment, the creation would fall into nothing.

Sermon 77, "Spiritual Worship," Works *6:426*

Reflections

God is sovereign and therefore God is able to care for and provide for all of creation.

In a world of almost instant communication and graphic story-telling about the tragedy and pain of the world, it is easy to forget this ancient truth.

Once we lose the concept of God as sovereign, our prayers, our faith, and our very souls begin to shrink. To believe in a severely limited God takes the heart out of reverence and out of prayer.

Commitment to a god that is too small will stifle any hope for a transformed world and dull our efforts to bring such a world into being. We become prisoners to our own weaknesses and the evil of the world when we forget that God is sovereign and God is able. Not only our salvation, but our prayers, our hope, our trust, our work, and our very lives are at risk when we follow a god too small to meet the needs of all of creation. Wesleyan theology never suffered from this weakness.

From the very beginning Wesley was clear about the sovereignty of God. He never doubted God's ability to care for and provide for all that God had created. God was omnipotent and there could never be any threat to God's power. Wesley did not minimize human responsibility but was always clear that God was sovereign and absolutely no worthy human endeavor could occur without God's participation. If God were to withhold participation, the creation itself would collapse.

Prayers that are completely dependent upon a sovereign God will touch the most troubling parts of our lives and society as a whole. Once we begin to incorporate belief in a sovereign God into our lives, we will be unafraid to throw our energies into the struggle that seems overwhelming without God. Fear, anxiety, and hopelessness are driven from our lives, for this sovereign God loves us and is able to care for us. We can live confidently and faithfully because God is able to care for and provide for all of creation.

Second Wesley Reading

> In a word, there is no point in space, whether within or without the bounds of creation, where God is not. Indeed, this subject is far too vast to be comprehended by the narrow limits of human understanding. We can only say, the great God, the eternal, the almighty Spirit, is as unbounded in his presence, as in his duration and power.
>
> *Sermon 111, "On the Omnipresence of God,"* Works 7:239

Time for Silent Reflection and Journaling

Blessing

> *The LORD will protect you on your journeys—*
> *whether going or coming—*
> *from now until forever from now.*
> *Psalm 121:8*

God Made Known

Prayer of Presence

Lover of all who are lost,
Uncertain and alone,
Confused and frightened,
Arrogant and disrespectful,
Anxious and fearful,
All who are seeking a safe and secure home,
And all who are already comfortably at home in your presence,
Come to me now and
Make yourself known to me
As I seek to quiet the noise of the world,
The anxiety of my heart and mind,
And the call of unfinished tasks
So that I may recognize and welcome your voice,
Embrace your presence,
Understand your call,
And invite you to change me more and more
Into that wonderful image you have of me
As your faithful, loving,
and obedient child. **Amen.**

Scripture

> *In the past, God spoke through the prophets to our ancestors*
> *in many times and many ways. In these final days, though,*
> *he spoke to us through a Son. God made his Son the heir of*
> *everything and created the world through him. The Son is*
> *the light of God's glory and the imprint of God's being. He*
> *maintains everything with his powerful message.*
>
> *Hebrews 1:1-3a*

First Wesley Reading

> Holiness is another of the attributes of the almighty, all-
> wise God. He is infinitely distant from every touch of evil.
> He "is light; and in him is no darkness at all." He is a God
> of unblemished justice and truth; but above all is his mercy.
> This we may easily learn from that beautiful passage in the
> thirty-third and fourth chapters of Exodus: "And Moses said,
> I beseech thee, show me thy glory. And the Lord descended
> in the cloud, and proclaimed the name of the Lord,—The
> Lord, The Lord God, merciful and gracious, longsuffering,
> and abundant in goodness and truth, keeping mercy for
> thousands, and forgiving iniquity and transgressions and sin."
>
> *Sermon 114, "The Unity of the Divine Being," Works 7:266*

Reflections

Despite our tendency sometimes to follow lesser gods, we know that, as
Christians, the God we profess is a particular God. We know that the call of
Jesus to follow him is a call to follow the God he lovingly called *Abba* and
to whom he fully gave his own life.

It is in Jesus that we have the clearest picture of who God is, what God does, and how God invites us to live as God's children.

The God Jesus reveals shatters all of our little ideas about God and reveals a God who is author and creator of all there is. In Jesus we see a God who reverses the values of our culture and turns upside down our scheme of priorities, leaving us gasping at the sight of such bone-deep love, justice, and mercy. In Jesus we see such bold and radical truth that we tremble in awe and then cry out for help as we try to practice the faithful way of living he demonstrated so splendidly.

In Jesus we see a God who is not swayed by popular opinion, loud adulation, or noisy rebellion. In Jesus we see clearly a God who is not controlled by any ideology, philosophy, concept, force, or power. In Jesus we see a God who is never under our control but always free of any control, and who may act and create as it seems wise and is in keeping with God's will.

Jesus reveals a God who is always and forever beyond us, completely other than who we are, and yet who wants to come and dwell within us (John 14:23). Jesus reveals a God of love.

Second Wesley Reading

> In a word, there is no point in space, whether within or without the bounds of creation, where God is not. Indeed, this subject is far too vast to be comprehended by the narrow limits of human understanding. We can only say, The great God, the eternal, the almighty Spirit, is as unbounded in his presence, as in his duration and power.
>
> *Sermon 111, "On the Omnipotence of God,"* Works *7:239*

Time for Silent Reflection and Journaling

Blessing

God of love beyond my comprehension, hold me close so that I may be as aware of the beat of your heart of love as I am of the beat of my own heart as you guide me through the day.

Seeking God

Prayer of Presence

> God! My God! It's you—
>   I search for you!
>   My whole being thirsts for you!
>   My body desires you
>   in a dry and tired land,
>   no water anywhere.
> Yes, I've seen you in the sanctuary;
>   I've seen your power and glory.
> My lips praise you
>   because your faithful love
>   is better than life itself!
> So I will bless you as long as I'm alive;
>   I will lift up my hands in your name.
>   Psalm 63:1-4

Scripture

> With what should I approach the LORD
>   and bow down before God on high?…

> *He has told you, human one, what is good and*
> *what the LORD requires from you:*
> > *to do justice, embrace faithful love, and walk humbly*
> > *with your God.*

Micah 6:6a, 8

First Wesley Reading

Almighty and everlasting God, the sovereign Lord of all creatures in heaven and earth, we acknowledge that our beings, and all the comforts of them, depend upon thee, the Fountain of all good. We have nothing but what is owing entirely to thy free and bounteous love, O most blessed Creator, and to the riches of thy grace, O most blessed Redeemer.

A Collection of Prayers for Families, Works *11:245*

Reflections

To love God with all of one's being was clearly an idea that captured the attention of John Wesley early and stayed with him to the end. He believed and practiced that loving God with all of the heart was the foundation for Christian living.

Faithfulness to God was a lifelong quest for the Wesley brothers. They learned from study and experience that this journey of faithfulness begins in the heart.

This quest of seeking God's presence and direction may seem overwhelming until we remember that Jesus told us we would have all the help we need in discovering what we must know in order to live fully as his disciples. He said, "The Companion, the Holy Spirit, whom the Father will send in my name, will teach you everything and will remind you of everything I told you" (John 14:26). We are not left on our own to learn how to pray or how to discern God's will; our Companion, the Holy Spirit, is our teacher and guide as we learn how to live more fully in relationship with God. It is God who chooses to make our way known to us, and it is God who does the revealing, leading, and instructing.

Second Wesley Reading

> We came in the evening to Boroughbridge, where, to my great surprise, the mistress of the house, though much of a gentlewoman, desired she and her family might join with us in prayer. They did so likewise between four and five in the morning. Perhaps even this seed may bring forth fruit.
>
> *Journal from May 31, 1742,* Works *1:374*

Time for Silent Reflection and Journaling

Blessing

> *Seek the LORD when he can still be found;*
> *call him while he is yet near.*
> *Let the wicked abandon their ways*
> *and the sinful their schemes.*
> *Let them return to the LORD so that he may have mercy on them,*
> *to our God because he is generous with forgiveness.*
>
> *Isaiah 55:6-7*

Three Simple Rules

- Do No Harm

- Do Good

- Stay in Love with God

Listening for God

Prayer of Presence

Holy God
   of unconditional love
   and unlimited presence,
   I come to make myself fully available
   to you, your will, and your way.
Speak to me gently and clearly,
   for I am yours
   and desire to hear, understand,
   and be obedient
   to your slightest whisper.
Speak, for I am listening.

Scripture

Six days later Jesus took Peter, James, and John his brother,
and brought them to the top of a very high mountain. He was
transformed in front of them. His face shone like the sun, and
his clothes became white as light.

Moses and Elijah appeared to them, talking with Jesus. Peter reacted to all of this by saying to Jesus, "Lord it's good that we're here. If you want, I'll make three shrines: one for you, one for Moses, and one for Elijah."

While he was still speaking, look, a bright cloud overshadowed them. A voice from the cloud said, "This is my Son whom I dearly love. I am very pleased with him. Listen to him!" Hearing this, the disciples fell on their faces, filled with awe.

Matthew 17:1-6

First Wesley Reading

When I was about twenty-two, my father pressed me to enter into holy orders. At the same time, the providence of God directing me to Kempis's "Christian Pattern," I began to see, that true religion was seated in the heart, and that God's law extended to all of our thoughts as well as words and actions. I was, however, very angry at Kempis, for being too strict; though I read him only in Dean Stanhope's translation. Yet I had frequently much sensible comfort in reading him, such as I was an utter stranger to before: And meeting likewise with a religious friend, which I had never had till now, I began to alter the whole form of my conversation, and set in earnest upon a new life. I set apart an hour or two a day for religious retirement. I communicated every week. I watched against all sin, whether in word or deed. I began to aim at, and pray for, inward holiness. So that now, "doing so much, and living so good a life," I doubted not but I was a good Christian.

Journal from May 4, 1738, Works 1:99

Reflections

Jesus often sought silence and solitude to pray and seek his beloved Abba's direction. No matter where we are in our busy and noisy world, we can do the same, but it will take practice, patience, and perseverance.

Our greatest challenge will be to learn to listen to the many ways in which God is speaking to us all the time—through Scripture, creation, history, current events, the stories of others and of our own lives, and the moments of our daily existence—and then to trust that the Holy Spirit desires to guide us as we learn how to pray and discern God's purpose and will for us in every situation. In other words, we will have the Master Teacher as our tutor for the rest of our lives—a teacher with all knowledge and compassion and the desire to see us live life fully, joyfully, productively, and faithfully.

John Wesley saw and experienced what we see and experience. It is impossible to live as a Christian if we are unattached to God. Our spiritual and even our physical lives become shambles without the constant companionship with God that prayer alone can make possible. Consequently, Wesley determined to be a man of ardent and consistent prayer. An exact replica of his disciplined life of prayer may not be possible for us, but I can be instructive as we fashion our own way of living with God in the world.

Second Wesley Reading

> Margaret Ropert, about eight years old, has been thoughtful for some time. The other day, while they were at family-prayer, she burst into tears and wept bitterly. They asked, what was the matter. She said she was a great sinner, and durst not pray. They bade her go to bed. She no sooner

came into the chamber than she began crying, and clapping her hands, so that they heard her across the street; but God soon bound up her broken heart. Being asked how she felt herself, she said, "Ten times better. Now I can love God. I wish you would sit up and sing with me all night." She has been happy ever since, and as serious as one of forty.

Journal from June 26, 1762, Works *3:105*

Time for Silent Reflection and Journaling

Blessing

God of love and compassion, grant me grace to walk in companionship with you this day so that I may hear and respond to your call and walk in faithfulness and peace this day and always.

Trusting God

Prayer of Presence

Loving God, I offer open hands, open mind, open heart, and a willing spirit to hear continually your calling and sending voice. I abandon my life and ministry into your care with the assurance that you will lead me in paths of righteousness and goodness. **Amen.**

Scripture

Let my whole being bless the Lord!
Let everything inside me bless his holy name!
Let my whole being bless the Lord
and never forget all his good deeds;
how God forgives all your sins,
heals all your sickness,
saves your life from the pit,
crowns you with faithful love and compassion,
and satisfies you with plenty of good things
so that your youth is made fresh like an eagle's.

The Lord works righteousness;
does justice for all who are oppressed.

God made his ways known to Moses;
made his deeds known to the Israelites.
The LORD is compassionate and merciful,
very patient, and full of faithful love.
God won't always play the judge;
he won't be angry forever.
He doesn't deal with us according to our sin
or repay us according to our wrongdoing
because as high as heaven is above the earth,
that's how large God's faithful love is for those who
honor him.

Psalm 103:1-11

First Wesley Reading

It is a divine evidence and conviction, Secondly, that what God hath promised he is able to perform. Admitting, therefore, that "with men it is impossible to bring a clean thing out of an unclean," to purify the heart from all sin, and to fill it with all holiness; yet this creates no difficulty in the case, seeing, "with God all things are possible." And surely no one ever imagined it was possible to any power less than that of the Almighty! But if God speaks, it shall be done. God saith, "Let there be light; and there" is "light!"

Sermon 43, "The Scripture Way of Salvation," Works 6:52

Reflections

To say that I am a Christian is really quite simple, but to live as a faithful follower of Jesus is another matter. Taking seriously the message of Jesus can be frightening and foreboding, because in my honest moments I know that on my own I cannot live the way of love that Jesus taught and lived. When I look at the immediate consequences of his life, I realize that the way of love is asking too much, and I am simply not up to living that way.

Then, like a fresh burst of wind, the realization breaks in upon me: I am not asked to do this on my own! I am asked to follow Jesus, and that means not only to do and be what Jesus calls me to do and be, but also to accept the power and presence of God to make me more than I am and enable me to live as a beloved child of God.

Wesley believed in and preached about a God who could never be touched by evil. The God that Jesus made known is light and there is no hint of darkness, no shadow of duplicity or falsehood to be found anywhere in God's being. Therefore God could never trick, injure, or lead even one person astray. This God always means all things for good for all. Mercy and steadfast love govern every relationship with humankind and every act in history.

Second Wesley Reading

> Do not take part of it for the whole! What God hath joined together, put not asunder! Take no less for his religion, than the "faith that worketh by love;" all inward and outward holiness. Be not content with any religion which does not imply the destruction of all the works of the devil; that is, of all sin. We know, weakness of understanding, and a thousand infirmities, will remain, while this corruptible body remains; but sin need not remain; This is that work of the devil, eminently so called, which the Son of God was manifested to destroy in the present life. He is able, he is willing, to

destroy it now, in all that believe in him....Do not distrust his power, or his love! Put his promise to the proof! He hath spoken: And is he not ready likewise to perform? Only "come boldly to the throne of grace," trusting in his mercy; and you shall find, "He saveth to the uttermost all those that come to God through him!"

Sermon 62, "The End of Christ's Coming," Works 6:277

Time for Silent Reflection and Journaling

Blessing

Remember your promise to your servant,
   for which you made me wait.
My comfort during my suffering is this:
   your word gives me new life.
                    Psalm 119:49-50

Living Prayerfully

Prayer of Presence

Loving God,
Who understands before I form my prayer,
Who hears when I call and translates my humble words
    into beautiful hymns of gratitude and praise
And responds to my uncertain cry for help
    with assurance, peace, and palpable presence,

Here I am as fully in your presence
    as I am able to be,
Offering my fears, my needs, my hopes,
    my love, and my life,
For I am yours and belong to no other.

Scripture

Brothers and sisters, we ask you to respect those who are
working with you, leading you, and instructing you. Think of
them highly with love because of their work. Live in peace with
each other. Brothers and sisters, we urge you to warn those

who are disorderly. Comfort the discouraged. Help the weak.
Be patient with everyone. Make sure no one repays a wrong
with a wrong, but always pursue the good for each other and
everyone else. Rejoice always. Pray continually. Give thanks in
every situation because this is God's will for you in Christ Jesus.
1 Thessalonians 5:12-18

First Wesley Reading

May it not be one of the consequences of this, that so many of you are a generation of triflers: triflers with God, with one another and with your own souls? For how few of you spend, from one week to another, a single hour in private prayer! How few have thought of God in the general tenor of your conversation! Who of you is, in any degree, acquainted with the work of the Spirit, his supernatural work in the souls of men?

Sermon 4, "Scriptural Christianity," Works 5:51

Reflections

Wesley knew that a life of prayer was not an accident or a natural consequence of just living. He was convinced that a life of prayer was the result of a determined and disciplined effort. He knew from personal experience that without this disciplined effort, prayer would become secondary and our relationship with God left to suffocate under the cares and delights of the world. So the disciplined life of prayer became a priority that he honored for his entire life.

Even a casual acquaintance with his journal will reveal that this disciplined life of prayer did not diminish his commitment to or involvement with the world of everyday cares and affairs. As a matter of fact, it seems clear that his involvement in the affairs of life received direction and power from the priority given to prayer.

John Wesley taught and lived a life of private, public, family, and community prayer. His earliest publishing venture was to provide direction and example for the person seeking to live a life of prayer. Prayers for families, children, clergy, the poor, prisoners, the sick, governmental and ecclesiastical authority, and prayers for self are found throughout his journal and sermons. Prayer was integral to his life.

Second Wesley Reading

> A Methodist is one who has "the love of God shed abroad in his heart by the Holy Ghost given unto him;" one who "loves the Lord his God with all his heart, and with all his soul, and with all his mind, and with all his strength."…But at all times the language of his heart is this: "Thou brightest of the eternal glory, unto thee is my heart, though without a voice, and my silence speaketh unto thee." And this is true prayer, and this alone. But his heart is ever lifted up to God, at all times and in all places. In this he is never hindered, much less interrupted, by any person or thing. In retirement or company, in leisure, business, or conversation, his heart is ever with the Lord. Whether he lie down or rise up, God is in all his thoughts; he walks with God continually, having the loving eye of his mind still fixed upon him, and everywhere "seeing Him that is invisible."
>
> *The Character of a Methodist,* Works *8:341, 343*

Time for Silent Reflection and Journaling

Blessing

I will accept and cherish my relationship as a beloved and loving child of God as I live a life of prayer in God's presence today.

Becoming a Prayerful People

Prayer of Presence

Loving Teacher, come and make your home in our hearts this day. Dwell within us all day long and save us from error or foolish ways. Teach us today to do no harm, to do good, and assist us so that we may stay in loving relationship with you and our neighbor. Help us today to be an answer to another's prayer so that we may be one of your signs of hope in the world you love.

Scripture

When you pray, don't pour out a flood of empty words, as the Gentiles do. They think that by saying many words they'll be heard. Don't be like them, because your Father knows what you need before you ask. Pray like this:

Our Father who is in heaven,
uphold the holiness of your name.
Bring in your kingdom
so that your will is done on earth as it's done in heaven.
Give us the bread we need for today.
Forgive us for the ways we have wronged you,

just as we also forgive those who have wronged us.
And don't lead us into temptation,
but rescue us from the evil one.

Matthew 6:7-13

First Wesley Reading

May we not endeavor, Secondly, to *instruct* them? to take care that every person who is under our roof have all such knowledge as is necessary to salvation?…and you should take care that they have some time every day for reading, meditation, and prayer; and you should inquire whether they do actually employ that time in the exercises for which it is allowed. Neither should any day pass without family prayer, seriously and solemnly performed.

Sermon 94, "On Family Religion," Works 7:81

Reflections

It is amazing that the disciples did not ask Jesus to teach them how to tell a parable, multiply the loaves, or heal the sick; but they did ask him to teach them how to pray. And when asked, Jesus taught them this simple and complete prayer. And the Lord's Prayer has been our pattern of prayer ever since. The disciples' request and the response of Jesus is more than a subtle reminder of the importance of prayer for them and for us. This brief prayer contains the essential elements of a healthy life of prayer and healthy relationship with the One to whom we pray.…

Becoming aware of God's presence, inviting God's intervention, listening for God's voice, making our requests known, offering ourselves to God, and receiving God's blessing are all essential elements in a faithful and fulfilling life with God. Our task is to weave them into the seamless garment of relationship with God that will sustain us in every experience of life and make it possible for us to live at home with God in this world and the next.

Prayer was so very important for Jesus that he left even the needy crowd to pray (Mark 6:31). It was so important to Wesley that he established a rigorous discipline of prayer, lest this lifeline to God be broken and life itself be lost.

Second Wesley Reading

> Serious and earnest prayer should be constantly used before we consult the oracles of God: seeing "Scripture can only be understood through the same Spirit whereby it was given." Our reading should likewise be closed with prayer, that what we read may be written on our hearts:…It might also be of use, if, while we read, we were frequently to pause and examine ourselves by what we read, both with regard to our hearts and lives. This would furnish us with matter of praise, where we found God had enabled us to conform to his blessed will; and matter of humiliation and prayer, where we were conscious of having fallen short. And whatever light you then receive should be used to the uttermost, and that immediately. Let there be no delay. Whatever you resolve, begin to execute the first moment you can. So shall you find this word to be indeed the power of God unto present and eternal salvation.

Works Abridged from Various Authors by John Wesley, Works *14:253*

Time for Silent Reflection and Journaling

Blessing

God of promise, power, and presence,
Be my ever-present Companion and Guide
So that this day and always
I may be your faithful servant child.

The Human Condition

Prayer of Presence

Loving God,
Remind me often today where I find my identity.
May I never forget that I am your beloved child.
May I listen for and hear your faintest whisper,
Feel your slightest touch,
Respond quickly to your call,
Yield to your word of correction,
Rejoice in your companionship,
And serve you faithfully all the days of my life.

Thank you for hearing my prayers
And accepting my life.
I offer them to you as completely as I can
In the Name and Spirit of Jesus Christ. **Amen**

Scripture

LORD, you have examined me.
You know me.

You know when I sit down and when I stand up.
　　Even from far away, you comprehend my plans.
You study my traveling and my resting.
　　You are thoroughly familiar with all my ways.
There isn't a word on my tongue, LORD,
　　that you don't already know completely.
You surround me—front and back.
　　You put your hand on me.
That kind of knowledge is too much for me;
　　it's so high above me that I can't fathom it.

You are the one who created my innermost parts;
　　you knit me together while I was still in my
　　mother's womb.
I give thanks to you that I was marvelously set apart.
　　Your works are wonderful—I know that very well.
My bones weren't hidden from you
　　when I was being put together in a secret place,
　　when I was being woven together in the deep parts of the earth.
Your eyes saw my embryo,
　　and on your scroll every day was written that was being
　　formed for me,
　　before any one of them had yet happened.
　　　　　　　　　　　　　　　　　　Psalm 139:1-6, 13-16

First Wesley Reading

For he created man in his own image: A spirit like himself;
a spirit endued with understanding, with will or affections,
and liberty; without which, neither his understanding nor

his affections could have been of any use, neither would he have been capable either of vice or virtue. He could not be a moral agent, any more than a tree or stone. If, therefore, God were thus to exert his power, there would certainly be no more vice; but it is equally certain, neither could there be any virtue in the world. Were human liberty taken away, men would be as incapable of virtue as stones. Therefore, (with reverence be it spoken) the Almighty himself cannot do this thing. He cannot thus contradict himself, or undo what he has done. He cannot destroy out of the soul of man that image of himself wherein he made him: And without doing this, he cannot abolish sin and pain out of the world. But were it to be done it would imply no wisdom at all; but barely a stroke of omnipotence. Whereas all the manifold wisdom of God (as well as all his power and goodness) is displayed in governing man as man; not as a stock or stone, but as an intelligent and free spirit, capable of choosing either good or evil.

Sermon 67, "On Divine Providence," Works *6:318*

Reflections

Sometimes I forget that I did not think of God first, love God first, decide to follow God first, or even decide to permit myself to be sent by God. None of this was my idea at all. It all came from God. Even before I was made, God loved me and had already chosen me. How could I be so arrogant as to think it was my idea all along? Perhaps it was and is my desire to be in charge, to be in control of my own destiny, when deep within I know so very well that I am completely dependent upon God for all things.

I think those first disciples and I have at least that much in common. They were each sought out by God in Christ and had to be reminded who they were, who it was that gave them life and loved them without limit, and who it was that chose them and sent them to be witnesses to the world. Even after three years with Jesus they needed each other and the power of the Holy Spirit to help them remember that they were indeed beloved, chosen and sent into the world by God.

We do love God because God first loved us. Our love is always in response to what God has done and is doing in our lives. Wesley was convinced that we could never love God or neighbor unless God had first loved us. Christians believe it is God in Christ who loves us and seeks and awakens our love in return. It is God who inspires and enables us to love our neighbor.

Second Wesley Reading

> While man is in a mere natural state, before he is born of God, he has, in a spiritual sense, eyes and sees not; a thick impenetrable veil lies upon them; he has ears, but hears not; he is utterly deaf to what he is most of all concerned to hear. His other spiritual senses are all locked up: He is in the same condition as if he had them not. Hence he has no knowledge of God; no intercourse with him; he is not at all acquainted with him. He has no true knowledge of the things of God, either of spiritual or eternal things; therefore, though he is a living man, he is a dead Christian. But as soon as he is born of God, there is a total change in all these particulars. The "eyes of his understanding are opened;" (such is the language of the great Apostle:) and, He who of old "commanded light to

shine out of darkness shining on his heart, he sees the light of the glory of God," his glorious love, "in the face of Jesus Christ." His ears being opened, he is now capable of hearing the inward voice of God, saying, "Be of good cheer; thy sins are forgiven thee:" "go and sin no more."

Sermon 45, "The New Birth," Works *6:70*

Time for Silent Reflection and Journaling

Blessing

We leave this time of prayer and reflection, remembering who we are as God's children and filled with confidence and peace because God is with us.

Do No Harm

The first simple rule is "Do no harm." It is not that complicated. And when practiced, it works wonders in transforming the world around us.

This first simple step, when practiced, can provide a safe place to stand while the hard and faithful work of discernment is done.

I will guard my lips, my mind and my heart so that my language will not disparage, injure or wound another child of God. I must do no harm, even while I seek a common good.

Remembering Who We Are

Prayer of Presence

Tender Shepherd,
Gather us in together as your flock,
Defend us from division,
Save us from sin,
Lead us in paths of righteousness, justice, peace, unity, and love,
Help us to discern wisely and well your will and way,
And grant us grace to follow faithfully
Wherever you may lead us,
For we are yours
And want to follow you alone.
Grant us grace to do so, we pray,
In the Name and Spirit of Jesus Christ,
Who taught us to pray....
"Our Father..." **Amen**.

Scripture

> *You are the salt of the earth. But if salt loses its saltiness, how*
> *will it become salty again? It's good for nothing except to be*

*thrown away and trampled under people's feet. You are the
light of the world. A city on top of a hill can't be hidden.
Neither do people light a lamp and put it under a basket.
Instead, they put it on top of a lampstand, and it shines on
all who are in the house. In the same way, let your light shine
before people, so they can see the good things you do and praise
your Father who is in heaven.*

Matthew 5:13-16

First Wesley Reading

But the most common of all the enthusiasts of this kind,
are those who imagine themselves Christians, and are not.
These abound, not only in all parts of our land, but in most
parts of the habitable earth. That they are not Christians
is clear and undeniable, if we believe the oracles of God.
For Christians are holy; these are unholy; Christians love
God; these love the world: Christians are humble, these are
proud; Christians are gentle; these are passionate; Christians
have the mind which was in Christ; these are at the utmost
distance from it. Consequently, they are no more Christians,
than they are archangels. Yet they imagine themselves so to
be; and they can give several reasons for it: For they have
been *called* so ever since they can remember; they were
christened many years ago; they embrace the *Christian
opinions*, vulgarly termed the Christian or Catholic faith;
they use the *Christian modes of worship*, as their fathers did
before them; they live what is called, a good *Christian life*,
as the rest of their neighbours do. And who shall presume

to think or say that these men are not Christians? – though without one grain of true faith in Christ, or of real inward holiness; without ever having tasted the love of God, or been "made partakers of the Holy Ghost!"

Sermon 37, "The Nature of Enthusiasm," Works 5:471

Reflections

At the center of our faith is the belief that we are not identified by our ancestors, our degrees, our pastoral appointments, or by the views of others. Our identity is found in the creator God who made us and in Jesus Christ who redeems us, transforms, sustains, and sends us to live faithful lives in the world that God loves (Eph. 1:1-23).

Clarity about who we are is found in God and in intimate companionship with God. This intimate companionship does not occur accidentally. It is the result of our consistent response to God's persistent invitation to relationship. And it is in this daily and intimate companionship that our identity as persons and pastors becomes clear.

The pressures to conform, to turn aside from our true identity, come not only from congregations and institutions. There are those inner needs that clamor for attention and lead us to seek and even create identity that is not founded in God. Even the pressure to conform can remind us who we are and to whom we belong.

The effort of the world to press all people into its mold is well known in our own culture and community. We hesitate to stand out, especially on faith or social issues. We are often timid in declaring our love for and faith in God and our love for and commitment to neighbor. It is easier to go along with popular opinion than to declare our own opinion that has grown out of deep, earnest, searching prayer.... From the beginning, Methodists felt called to live out their faith in practical ways—ways that brought healing and wholeness to individuals and to the human family.

Second Wesley Reading

> In the evening we came to Stafford. The mistress of the house joined with us in family prayer. The next morning one of the servants appeared deeply affected, as did the ostler before we went. Soon after breakfast, stepping into the stable, I spake a few words with those who were there. A stranger who heard me said, "Sir I wish I was to travel with you:" and when I went into the house, followed me, and began abruptly, "Sir, I believe you are a good man, and I come to tell you a little of my life." The tears stood in his eyes all the time he spoke; and we hoped not a word which was said to him was lost.
>
> *Journal from March 15, 1738,* Works *1:87*

Time for Silent Reflection and Journaling

Blessing

God of love, mercy, and peace, pour out your Spirit upon us to form and transform our lives more and more into your grand design for us all.

A World of Darkness

Prayer of Presence

Save me, God,
> because the waters have reached my neck!
I have sunk into deep mud.
> My feet can't touch the bottom!
I have entered deep water;
> the flood has swept me up.
I am tired of crying.
> My throat is hoarse.
> My eyes are exhausted with waiting for my God.

Save me from the mud!
> Don't let me drown!
> Let me be saved from those who hate me
> and from these watery depths!
Don't let me be swept away by the floodwaters!
> Don't let the abyss swallow me up!
> Don't let the pit close its mouth over me!
Answer me, LORD, for your faithful love is good!
> Turn to me in your great compassion!

Don't hide your face from me, your servant,
because I'm in deep trouble.
Answer me quickly!
Come close to me!
Redeem me!
Save me because of my enemies!
Psalm 69:1-3, 14-18

Scripture

In the beginning was the Word
and the Word was with God
and the Word was God.
The Word was with God in the beginning.
Everything came into being through the Word,
and without the Word
nothing came into being.
What came into being
through the Word was life,
and the life was the light for all people.
The light shines in the darkness,
and the darkness doesn't extinguish the light.
John 1:1-5

First Wesley Reading

It has been frequently supposed, that there is another cause if not of darkness, at least, of heaviness; namely, God's withdrawing himself from the soul, because it is his sovereign will. Certainly he will do this, if we grieve his Holy Spirit, either by outward or inward sin; either by doing evil, or neglecting to do good; by giving way either to pride or anger, to spiritual sloth, to foolish desire, or inordinate affection. But that he ever withdraws himself *because he will*, merely because it is his good pleasure, I absolutely deny. There is no text in all the Bible which gives any colour for such a supposition. Nay, it is a supposition contrary, not only to many particular texts, but to the whole tenor of Scripture. It is repugnant to the very nature of God: It is utterly beneath his majesty and wisdom, (as an eminent writer strongly expresses it,) "to play at bo-peep with his creatures." It is inconsistent with both his justice and mercy, and with the sound experience of all his children.

Sermon 47, "Heaviness Through Manifold Temptation," Works 6:98

Reflections

Ours was a dark and frightening world when God sent light and life through the birth of a child....God sent Jesus, the Word, into our dark world to bring life, light, hope, healing and peace. Yet today much of the world still lies in darkness. Of course, there is unprecedented wealth and pleasure for a few; but a multitude of God's children live in the darkness of disease, disaster, hunger, poverty, oppression, and violence. The vast majority of our sisters and brothers struggle every day just to survive.

Far too often we witness national and global tragedies that result in the death and wounding of many. We have also seen political leaders divide communities, states, and nations by their rhetoric and actions. It is not a time to offer excuses or to place blame. But it is time for all Christians to remember who we are and to chart and follow a new path—a path that always moves away from violence and toward peace, a path that leads us away from the implied and symbolic threat of much of our national discourse, a path that affirms finding a way forward that benefits all and not just a few, a path that is in harmony with the One we claim as Lord and Savior, Jesus Christ, a path that I believe we all want to follow.

No one is ever outside the reach of God's loving presence. Even though we may try to place ourselves beyond the gaze of God, the psalmist reminds us it is impossible:

> *If I ascend to heaven, you are there;*
> *if I make my bed in Sheol, you are there.*
> *If I take the wings of the morning*
> *and settle at the farthest limits of the sea,*
> *even there your hand shall lead me,*
> *and your right hand shall hold me fast.*
> *Psalm 139:8-10 NRSV*

Not only is it impossible to step outside God's gracious reach but God is always actively engaged on our behalf. God's right hand does hold us fast, no matter how far we stray from God's grand design for us, a design that was in place even before the foundation of the world. (See Ephesians 1:4-5.)

It was the conviction of God's preventing grace (often referred to as prevenient grace today) that led John Wesley to believe that everyone had within them this mark of divinity that could not be extinguished. He believed that God is active on our behalf and in our lives whether we recognize it or not.

Second Wesley Reading

> For allowing that all the souls of men are dead in sin by nature, this excuses none, seeing there is no man that is in a state of mere nature; there is no man, unless he has quenched

the Spirit, that is wholly void of the grace of God. No man living is entirely destitute of what is vulgarly called *natural conscience*. But this is not natural: It is more properly termed, *preventing grace*. Every man has a greater or less measure of this, which waiteth not for the call of man. Every one has, sooner or later, good desires; although the generality of men stifle them before they can strike deep root, or produce any considerable fruit. Every one has some measure of that light, some faint glimmering ray, which, sooner or later, more or less, enlightens every man that cometh into the world. And every one, unless he be one of the small number whose conscience is seared with a hot iron, feels more or less uneasy when he acts contrary to the light of his own conscience. So that no man sins because he has not grace, but because he does not use the grace which he hath.

Sermon 85, "On Working Out Our Own Sanctification," Works 6:512

Time for Silent Reflection and Journaling

Blessing

> *The salvation of the righteous comes from the LORD;*
> *he is their refuge in times of trouble.*
> *The LORD will help them and rescue them—*
> *rescue them from the wicked—and he will save them*
> *because they have taken refuge in him.*
>
> *Psalm 37:39-40*

Keeping Close to Grace

Keep close, I beseech you,
to every means of grace.
Strive to walk in all the ordinances
and commandments of God blameless...
"Add to your faith virtue;
to virtue knowledge;
to knowledge temperance;
to temperance patience;
to patience godliness;
to godliness...kindness;
to...kindness charity."

God's Beloved Children

Prayer of Presence

The LORD is my shepherd,
  I lack nothing.
He lets me rest in grassy meadows;
  he leads me to restful waters;
    he keeps me alive.
He guides me in proper paths
  for the sake of his good name.

Even when I walk through the darkest valley,
  I fear no danger because you are with me,
Your rod and your staff—
  they protect me.

You set a table for me
  right in front of my enemies,
You bathe my head in oil;
  my cup is so full it spills over!

Yes, goodness and faithful love
will pursue me all the days of my life,
and I will live in the LORD's house
as long as I live.

Psalm 23

Scripture

See what kind of love the Father has given to us in that we
should be called God's children, and that is what we are!
Because the world didn't recognize him, it doesn't recognize us.

Dear friends now we are God's children, and it hasn't yet
appeared what we will be. We know that when he appears we
will be like him because we'll see him as he is. And everyone
who has this hope in him purifies himself even as he is pure.

1 John 3:1-3

First Wesley Reading

You, to whom I now speak, believe this love of human kind
cannot spring but from the love of God. You think there can
be no instance of one whose tender affection embraces every
child of man, (though not endeared to him either by ties of
blood, or by any natural or civil relation,) unless that affection
flow from a grateful, filial love to the common Father of all;
to God, considered not only as his Father, but as "the Father
of the spirits of all flesh;" yea, as the general Parent and
Friend of all the families both of heaven and earth.

Advice to the People Called Methodists, Works *8:352*

Reflections

The god we worship is often too small to meet the demands of our lives, much less the demands of our violent and needy world. The Bible speaks often of a God for whom all things are possible. We all seek a God who is competent to deal with the needs of the entire creation. A god who is captive to the creation or to any other power is not God at all. The biblical witness is about a God who is omnipotent and transcendent....

While such an almighty and transcendent God is part of the biblical witness, it is not the entire story.... Jesus describes God as a loving parent who seeks to gather humankind and hold each and all as close as a mother hen gathers and protects her chicks beneath her wings. He also described God as a waiting father, generous to all of his children who have chosen to live with him and yet anxiously seeking the lost one—never content until all have come home. The waiting father continually yearns for those who are far away and seeks them out, woos them with love, persuades them with hope, and persistently encourages their return.

These two streams of theological thought and practice are an integral part of our Methodist heritage. Methodists believe in a God for whom nothing is impossible. Therefore we are bold enough to pray for the unthinkable, from the healing of a child to the peace of the world. We are bold enough and full of enough faith to throw our every energy, our very lives, into the battle for justice and goodness....

Methodists also believe in a God who is seeking relationship and companionship with each of us. God calls each of us by name and knows our most intimate secrets and our most horrible fears. And yet we are gathered in divine embrace because, as the scripture says, we have "found favor" with God.

Second Wesley Reading

> O the tender care of Almighty God in bringing up his children! How are we bound to love so indulgent a Father, and to fall down in wonder and adoration of his great and glorious name, for his tender mercies!
>
> *Journal from December 3, 1744,* Works 1:478

Time for Silent Reflection and Journaling

Blessing

This day we claim the promise, presence, and power of God to bring us to our full humanity, whole and happy as God's beloved children.

Our New Nature

Prayer of Presence

God of love and compassion, author of life and all creation, we now offer ourselves to you and invite your presence fully into our lives to mold and shape us, as a skilled potter brings forth something good, useful, and beautiful from malleable clay.

Scripture

So, since we have such a hope, we act in confidence. We aren't like Moses, who used to put a veil over his face so that the Israelites couldn't watch the end of what was fading away. But their minds were closed. Right up to the present day the same veil remains when the old covenant is read. The veil is not removed because it is taken away by Christ. Even today, whenever Moses is read, a veil lies over their hearts. But whenever someone turns back to the Lord, the veil is removed. The Lord is the Spirit, and where the Lord's Spirit is, there is freedom. All of us are looking with unveiled faces at the glory of the Lord as if we were looking in a mirror. We are being transformed into that same image from one degree of glory to

the next degree of glory. This comes from the Lord who is the
Spirit.

2 Corinthians 3:12-18

First Wesley Reading

Men are generally lost in the hurry of life, in the business or pleasures of it, and seem to think that their regeneration, their new nature, will spring and grow up within them, with as little care and thought of their own as their bodies were conceived and have attained their full strength and stature; whereas, there is nothing more certain than that the Holy Spirit will not purify our nature, unless we carefully attend to his motions, which are lost upon us while, in the Prophet's language, we "scatter away our time,"—while we squander away our thoughts upon unnecessary things and leave our spiritual improvement, the one thing needful, quite unthought of and neglected.

Sermon 138, "On Grieving the Holy Spirit," Works 7:489

Reflections

At this very moment, whoever and wherever you are, something beyond our full comprehension is taking place within your life and mine. The infinite God of love has chosen to become resident within you and to work within you for pure good. Since God is pure goodness and has no ulterior motives, we can trust, embrace, and cooperate with the divine work going on within us and every child of God.

Once we accept this truth and fully embrace this Divine Presence within us, many other things become clear and possible. We can listen to and follow the guidance of the One who made us, loves us, and is able to lead us in the way of God. We can hear and respond to the Divine call to communion and community with the present and living God. We can hear and respond to faithfulness and service because we are no longer on our own, but the power and the presence of the God at work within us is ready, available, and capable to form, transform, and shape us into the beautiful, faithful, and good persons we were created to become. We can now walk through each day without fear because we remember that we do not walk alone but always with the companionship and help of the One who is now at work within us.

Second Wesley Reading

> Our coming to Christ…must infer a great and mighty change. It must infer not only an *outward change*, from stealing, lying, and all corrupt communication; but a thorough *change of heart*, and *inward* renewal in the spirit of our mind. Accordingly, "the old man" implies infinitely more than outward evil conversation, even "an evil heart of unbelief," corrupted by pride and a thousand deceitful lusts. Of consequence, the "new man" must imply infinitely more than outward good conversation, even "a good heart, which after God is created in righteousness and true holiness," a heart full of that faith which, working by love, produces all holiness of conversation.
>
> *Journal from July 31, 1739,* Works *1:214*

Time for Silent Reflection and Journaling

Blessing

> His understanding is beyond human reach,
>   giving power to the tired
>   and reviving the exhausted.
> Youths will become tired and weary
>   young men will certainly stumble;
>   but those who hope in the LORD
>   will renew their strength;
>   they will fly up on wings like eagles;
>   they will run and not be tired;
>   they will walk and not be weary.
>   *Isaiah 40:28c-31*

The Way of Love

Prayer of Presence

O Divine Love, who calls and sends all who follow you, help me in this time apart to once more hear your voice. Grant grace to hear your voice calling and sending me, and grant faith enough to respond in obedience. **Amen.**

Scripture

As the Father loved me, I too have loved you. Remain in my love. If you keep my commandments, you will remain in my love, just as I have kept my Father's commandments and remain in his love. I have said these things to you so that my joy will be in you and your joy will be complete. This is my commandment: love each other just as I have loved you. No one has greater love than to give up one's life for one's friends. You are my friends if you do what I command you. I don't call you servants any longer, because servants don't know what their master is doing. Instead, I call you friends, because everything I heard from my Father I have made known to you. You didn't choose me, but I chose you and appointed you so that you could go and produce fruit and so that your fruit

could last. As a result, whatever you ask the Father in my
name, he will give you. I give you these commandments so that
you can love each other.

John 15:9-17

First Wesley Reading

Are you a witness of the religion of love? Are you a lover of God and all mankind? Does your heart glow with gratitude to the Giver of every good and perfect gift....Do you "walk in love, as Christ also loved us, and gave himself for us?" Do you, as you have time, "do good unto all men:" and in as high a degree as you are able?...Whosoever thou art, whose heart is herein as my heart, give me thine hand! Come and let us magnify the Lord together, and labour to promote his kingdom upon the earth! Let us join hearts and hands in this blessed work, in striving to bring glory to God in the highest, by establishing peace and good will among men, to the uttermost of our power!

Sermon 132, "On Laying the Foundation of the New Chapel,"
Works 7:430

Reflections

Living in community is not easy. Sometimes we are able to live together faithfully only when we remember that God is there with us, and that it is God's love that binds us together into the body of Christ.

As Christians, we worship and seek to follow the God of Abraham and Isaac; the God of Mary and Elizabeth; the God of Matthew, James, and John; the God of prophets and saints of every age; and the God made known most clearly in the life, death, and resurrection of Jesus Christ. In Jesus we have the best picture of who God is, how God acts in the world, and how God relates to us. In Jesus we discover the truth that you and I are God's beloved children, just like every other person on this good earth. We not only are "authored" by God; we are sustained by God every moment of our existence. Our destiny is to live in confidence and trust in loving relationship with this mighty God and with our neighbors—with all God's children—who are just like you and me. When we live this way, we begin to love as God loves; we begin to love our neighbors as we love ourselves.

The essential nature of the Christian faith and life is love. All else revolves around this vital center, God's love for us and our awakened love for God and neighbor. And this love is most profoundly, clearly, and simply revealed in the life, death, and resurrection of Jesus Christ. John Wesley's journal, letters, sermons, and biblical commentary all reflect this center for his thought and faith.

Second Wesley Reading

> That the testimony of the Spirit of God must, in the very nature of things, be antecedent to the testimony of our own spirit, may appear from this single consideration: We must be holy in heart and life before we can be conscious that we are so. But we must love God before we can be holy at all, this being the root of all holiness. Now we cannot love God, till we know he loves us: "We love him, because he first loved us:" And we cannot know his love to us, till his Spirit witnesses it to our spirit. Till then we cannot believe it; we

cannot say, "The life which I now live, I live by faith in the son of God, who loved me, and gave himself for me."

Sermon 11, "The Witness of the Spirit," Works 5:127

Time for Silent Reflection and Journaling

Blessing

Dear friends, let's love each other, because love is from God, and everyone who loves is born of God and knows God.

1 John 4:7

Life in Christ

Prayer of Presence

Faithful Guide and Companion, continue to speak to me the words of guidance, correction, encouragement, and love that I need. And send me to meet this day with your power and presence to go where Jesus Christ leads me and live as your faithful disciple all day long.

Scripture

When Jesus arrived, he found that Lazarus had already been in the tomb for four days. Bethany was a little less than two miles from Jerusalem. Many Jews had come to comfort Martha and Mary after their brother's death. When Martha heard that Jesus was coming, she went to meet him, while Mary remained in the house. Martha said to Jesus, "Lord, if you had been here, my brother wouldn't have died. Even now I know that whatever you ask God, God will give you."

Jesus told her, "Your brother will rise again."

Martha replied, "I know that he will rise in the resurrection on the last day."

Jesus said to her, "I am the resurrection and the life. Whoever believes in me will live, even though they die. Everyone who lives and believes in me will never die. Do you believe this?"

She replied, "Yes, Lord, I believe that you are the Christ, God's Son, the one who is coming into the world."

John 11:17-27

First Wesley Reading

How different is the case, how vast the pre-eminence, of them that "walk by faith"! God, having "opened the eyes of their understanding," pours divine light into their soul: whereby they are enabled to "see Him that is invisible," to see God and the things of God. What their "eye had not seen, nor their ear heard, neither had it entered into their heart to conceive." God from time to time reveals to them by the "unction of the Holy One, which teacheth them of all things." Having "entered into the holiest by the blood of Jesus," by that "new and living way," and being joined into "the general assembly and church of the first born, and unto God the Judge of all, and Jesus the Mediator of the New Covenant,"—each of these can say, "I live not, but Christ liveth in me:" I now live that life which "is hid with Christ in God," "and when Christ, who is my life, shall appear, then I shall likewise appear with him in glory."

Sermon 113, "Walking by Faith," Works 7:260

Reflections

Jesus declared, "I am the bread of life. Whoever comes to me will never be hungry, and whoever believes in me will never be thirsty" (John 6:35)....

Why then is it so hard to see this life abundant and eternal reflected in the church and in the lives of individual Christians? John Wesley seemed to believe that the answer is quite simple. We have not really feasted on the bread of life and we have not yet given ourselves completely to God in Christ....

To live in Christ is to give all that we are, have, and hope to become to God's gracious direction. This is to enter into "fellowship" with God in a new and nurturing way—a way that leads to assurance of salvation and life abundant and eternal. It is a way that leads to the confidence and comfort that only companionship with Jesus Christ can bring. And it is a way that leads to definite and decisive response on the part of the believer.

In a world where institutions and individuals seem to be unworthy of trust, the believer finds in God one who is completely trustworthy. Thus it is possible to offer one's life, without reservation, and as totally as we are able, to this trustworthy God. Because God can be trusted, we can give ourselves to God without fear or anxiety that we will be deceived or disappointed. This kind of trust leads more and more to the living out of our faith. Life in Christ not only brings assurance and hope, it also begins to show some of the characteristics of Christ within the life of the believer. It is to have the image of God within each of us restored and made visible to ourselves and to others.

We have often seen children take on the qualities of their parents and students begin to reflect in their lives the life and ways of their teachers. To live in an intimate relationship with Christ is to begin to act like Christ, to think like Christ, and to be Christ-like in all of our living. Life in Christ brings great gifts that so many times are left unclaimed by those of us who start the Christian journey but are quick to turn away from the fullness of life that is offered. Our inheritance of assurance, comfort, and peace, life abundant and eternal is often not incorporated into our daily life. Because it is not, we live anxious, fearful and incomplete lives, and we begin to wonder what difference our faith really makes. Life in Christ changes all of that as we live in the presence and power of Jesus Christ.

A further consequence of life in Christ is the pursuit of the way of Christ. We seek to be faithful and obedient as Jesus Christ was obedient. We observe more closely the life of Jesus and try to incorporate his ways into our own. As we do this, we learn to love God and realize that we cannot truly love God without loving our neighbor.

Second Wesley Reading

> And it is as impossible to satisfy such a soul, a soul that is athirst for God, the living God, with what the world accounts religion, as with what they account happiness. The religion of the world implies three things: (1) The doing no harm, the abstaining from outward sin; at least from such as is scandalous, as robbery, theft, common swearing, drunkenness: (2) The doing good, the relieving the poor; the being charitable, as it is called: (3) The using of the means of grace; at least the going to church and to the Lord's Supper. He in whom these three marks are found is termed by the world a religious man. But will this satisfy him who hungers after God? No: It is not food for his soul. He wants a religion of a nobler kind, a religion higher and deeper than this....

> This is only the outside of that religion, which he insatiably hungers after. The knowledge of God in Christ Jesus: "the life which is hid with Christ in God:" the being "joined unto the Lord in one spirit:" the having "fellowship with the Father and the Son:" the "walking in the light as God is in

the light:" the being "purified even as He is pure:"—this is the religion, the righteousness, he thirsts after: Nor can he rest, till he thus rests in God.

Sermon 22, "Sermon on the Mount, Discourse 2," Works 5:268

Time for Silent Reflection and Journaling

Blessing

May grace and peace rest upon us to guide, strengthen, and keep us as we seek to follow the way of Christ. May it be so today and always.

Do Good

Doing good, like doing no harm,
is a proactive way of living.

I do not need to wait to be
asked to do some good deed
or provide some needed help.

I do not need to wait until circumstances
cry out for aid to relieve suffering
or correct some horrible injustice.

I can decide that my way of living will
come down on the side of doing good to
all in every circumstance and in
every way I can.

I can decide that I will choose a way
of living that nourishes goodness
and strengthens community

Holiness of Heart

Prayer of Presence

> Have mercy on me, God, according to your faithful love!
>> Wipe away my wrongdoings according to your great
>> compassion!
> Wash me completely clean of my guilt;
>> purify me from my sin!
> Because I know my wrongdoings,
>> my sin is always right in front of me....
>
> Create a clean heart for me, God;
>> put a new, faithful spirit deep inside me!
>
> Psalm 51:1-3, 10

Scripture

> Now these are the commandments, the regulations, and the
> case laws that the LORD your God commanded me to teach
> you to follow in the land you are entering to possess, so that
> you will fear the LORD your God by keeping all his regulations
> and his commandments that I am commanding you—both

you and your sons and daughters—all the days of your life
and so that you will lengthen your life. Listen to them, Israel!
Follow them carefully so that things will go well for you and so
that you will continue to multiply exactly as the LORD, your
ancestors' God, promised you, in a land full of milk and honey.

Israel, listen! Our God is the LORD! Only the LORD!

Love the LORD your God with all your heart, all your being,
and all your strength. These words that I am commanding
you today must always be on your minds. Recite them to your
children. Talk about them when you are sitting around your
house and when you are out and about, when you are lying
down and when you are getting up. Tie them on your hand
as a sign. They should be on your forehead as a symbol. Write
them on your house's doorframes and on your city's gates.

Deuteronomy 6:1-9

First Wesley Reading

Now, "this word is nigh thee." This condition of life is plain,
easy, always at hand. "It is in thy mouth, and in thy heart,"
through the operation of the Spirit of God. The moment
"thou believest in thine heart" in him whom God "hath
raised from the dead," and "confessest with thy mouth the
Lord Jesus" as *thy* Lord and *thy* God, "thou shalt be saved"
from condemnation, from the guilt and punishment of
thy former sins, and shalt have power to serve God in true
holiness all the remaining days of thy life.

Sermon 6, "The Righteousness of Faith," Works 5:69

Reflections

Holiness is an uncommon word in our vocabulary, but it was a central word and concept in the life and teaching of John Wesley. The seed was likely planted by his mother and was nurtured through a lifetime of study and seeking to be obedient to the will of God in every aspect of life.

To love God with all of one's being was clearly an idea that captured the attention of John Wesley early and stayed with him to the end. He believed and practiced that loving God with all of the heart was the foundation for all other Christian living.

Inward and outward holiness are inseparable because all actions and attitudes find their root in the heart. Thus a holy, pure, committed heart will lead to a life that reflects this holiness in all aspects and activities of the daily journey. Holiness of heart is a prerequisite that leads unquestionably to holiness of life.

When we follow such a course we discover that without a heart given to God, even our efforts at reflecting God's light are often hopelessly inadequate. Only when God in Christ is embraced as only Savior, only Lord, and only necessary companion in all of life, only then can our outward actions be trusted to reflect God's light.

Faithfulness to God was a lifelong quest for the Wesley brothers. They learned from study and experience that this journey of faithfulness begins in the heart. When the heart is holy, all of life is transformed. God is holy and we depend upon God's grace to travel the road toward a holy heart.

Holiness of heart opens us to the direction of the Holy Spirit, gives the assurance of sins forgiven and life held close and secure in the hands of God. Holiness of heart is the beginning, but as we shall see, there is much more to come.

Second Wesley Reading

He, therefore, who liveth in true believers, hath "purified their hearts by faith:" insomuch that every one that hath Christ in him the hope of glory, "purifieth himself, even as He is pure." (1 John 3:3) He is purified from pride; for Christ was lowly of heart. He is pure from self will or desire; for Christ desired only to do the will of his Father, and to finish his work. And he is pure from anger, in the common sense of the word; for Christ was meek and gentle, patient and longsuffering.

Sermon 40, "Christian Perfection," Works 6:17

Time for Silent Reflection and Journaling

Blessing

Teach me your way, LORD,
so that I can walk in your truth.
Make my heart focused
only on honoring your name.
Psalm 86:11

God's Grace

Prayer of Presence

God of love, holiness, and strength, we thank you for the gift of your presence through the morning hours. Continue to make yourself and your way known to us throughout the remaining hours of the day. Grant us grace to follow you in faithfulness, joy, and peace. We are yours.

Scripture

Therefore, since we have been made righteous through his faithfulness, we have peace with God through our Lord Jesus Christ. We have access by faith into this grace in which we stand through him, and we boast in the hope of God's glory. But not only that! We even take pride in our problems, because we know that trouble produces endurance, endurance produces character, and character produces hope. This hope doesn't put us to shame, because the love of God has been poured out in our hearts through the Holy Spirit, who has been given to us.

While we were still weak, at the right moment, Christ died for ungodly people. It isn't often that someone will die for a *righteous person, though maybe someone might dare to die for a good person. But God shows his love for us, because while we were still sinners Christ died for us.…*

If we were reconciled to God through the death of his Son while we were still enemies, now that we have been reconciled, how much more certain is it that we will be saved by his life? And not only that: we even take pride in God through our Lord Jesus Christ, the one through whom we now have a restored relationship with God.

Romans 5:1-8, 10-11

First Wesley Reading

One more thing is implied in this repentance; namely, a conviction of our helplessness, or our utter inability to think one good thought, or to form one good desire; and much more to speak one word aright, or to perform one good action, but through his free almighty grace first preventing us, and then accompanying us every moment.

Sermon 43, "The Scripture Way of Salvation," Works 6:51

Reflections

The Christian life is impossible without God's grace extended to the believer. God is the seeker and always initiates every relationship with us. Even our awakening to God is a response to the Holy Spirit at work within us. God may choose to come to us, save us, provide for us, and hold us close to the divine in any way God chooses. We cannot control the ways or means that God will choose to use in our transformation any more than we can command God to transform us. However, we can choose to utilize those means of grace that have consistently been used by God to draw persons toward goodness and God. And unless we utilize these channels of sustenance, it is unlikely that we will experience the joy or fruit of discipleship.

Wesley believed that the grace of God was freely offered to all, and he believed that God used the means of grace to offer the fruits of grace to every believer. Therefore, no one had to suffer from unforgiven sin. No one had to walk alone. No one had to be a prisoner of fear. No one had to stay as she or he was. All could know sins forgiven. All could know the assurance and comfort of the Savior's presence in their lives. All could be redeemed and all could, by God's grace, travel the road to perfection. It was grace, God's grace, that made all of this possible.

Living in the presence of and in harmony with the living God who is made known in Jesus Christ and companions us in the Holy Spirit is to live life from the inside out. It is to find our moral direction, our wisdom, our courage, our strength to live faithfully from the One who authored us, called us, sustains us, and sends us into the world as witnesses who daily practice the way of living with Jesus.

It is impossible to stay in love with God and not desire to see God's goodness and grace shared with the entire world.

Second Wesley Reading

> Several of these, after being thoroughly sensible of their fall, and deeply ashamed before God, have been again filled with his love, and not only perfected therein, but stablished, strengthened, and settled. They have received the blessing they had before with abundant increase. Nay, it is

remarkable, that many who had fallen either from justifying or from sanctifying grace, and so deeply fallen that they could hardly be ranked among the servants of God, have been restored, (but seldom till they had been shaken, as it were, over the mouth of hell,) and that very frequently in an instant, to all that they had lost. They have, at once, recovered both a consciousness of his favour, and the experience of the pure love of God. In one moment they received anew both remission of sins, and a lot among them that were sanctified.

Sermon 86, "A Call to Backsliders," Works 6:526

Time for Silent Reflection and Journaling

Blessing

May God's grace and peace be multiplied to you.
1 Peter 1:2b

Prevenient Grace

Prayer of Presence

> It is good to give thanks to the LORD,
>> to sing praises to your name, Most High;
>> to proclaim your loyal love in the morning,
>>> your faithfulness at nighttime....
>> because you've made me happy, LORD,
>> by your acts.
>> I sing with joy because of your handiwork.
>>>> Psalm 92:1-2, 4

Scripture

> "I didn't say these things to you from the beginning, because
> I was with you. But now I go away to the one who sent me.
> None of you ask me, 'Where are you going?' Yet because I have
> said these things to you, you are filled with sorrow. I assure
> you that it is better for you that I go away. If I don't go away,
> the Companion won't come to you. But if I go, I will send
> him to you. When he comes, he will show the world it was
> wrong about sin, righteousness, and judgment. He will show

*the world it was wrong about sin because they don't believe in
me. He will show the world it was wrong about righteousness
because I'm going to the Father and you won't see me anymore.
He will show the world it was wrong about judgment because
this world's ruler stands condemned.*

*"I have much more to say to you, but you can't handle it now.
However, when the Spirit of Truth comes, he will guide you in
all truth. He won't speak on his own, but will say whatever he
hears and will proclaim to you what is to come. He will glorify
me, because he will take what is mine and proclaim it to you.
Everything that the Father has is mine. That's why I said that
the Spirit takes what is mine and will proclaim it to you.*

John 16:4b-15

First Wesley Reading

At what time I became a subject to my own will, I cannot
ascertain; but from that time in many things I offended.
First, against my parents; next, against God! And that I was
preserved from outward evils, was not owing to the purity
of my own will; but the grace of Christ preventing and
overruling me.

Journal from June 24, 1763, Works 3:140

Reflections

It was the conviction of God's preventing grace (often called prevenient
grace today) that led John Wesley to believe that everyone had within them

[a] mark of divinity that could not be extinguished. He believed that God is active on our behalf and in our lives whether we recognize it or not.

Our lives are shaped by the God we worship. If we give allegiance to an absent, cool, distant, and uncaring God, we may feel cut off, alone, unprotected, and uncared for. On the other hand, if we worship a God who loves us without condition, walks with us even when we deny Divine Presence, who is actively engaged for the good of all humankind (even me), we will find an assurance, peace, and joy in every condition of life that we experience.

Most mature Christians look back at their lives and see that God has indeed prevented them from painful mistakes, kept them from unworthy goals, and guided them and events around them, even though they were unaware of God's nearness and intervention on their behalf. They also testify that God apprehended *them*, rather than the other way around. It was God who sought them out, wooed their attention, and called forth their love.

It is this awakening call, this divine spark within, this active involvement in all of life that today is called prevenient grace. And it is this unmerited action of God within and without that makes it possible for us to respond to God, know God, and walk in companionship with God. Each one of us is this very moment experiencing the active involvement of God within our lives and on our behalf in the world in which we live. Were God to withhold this grace, we would no longer *be*. It is this grace of God that calls forth our own response of love, faith and desire to walk with God in Christ. Today, in more ways than we will ever know, God is seeking our response. What shall we do? John Wesley and countless Christians before and after him would say, "Repent, believe, and offer your life to God in Christ anew this very moment." This is the appropriate and faithful response to God's prevenient grace.

Second Wesley Reading

> If we take this in its utmost extent, it will include all that is wrought in the soul by what is frequently termed natural conscience, but more properly, preventing grace:—all the drawings of the Father; the desires after God, which, if we yield to them, increase more and more:—all that light wherewith the Son of God "enlighteneth every one that cometh into the world:" showing every man "to do justly, to love mercy, and to walk humbly with his God:"—all the convictions which his Spirit, from time to time, works in every child of man; although, it is true, the generality of men stifle them as soon as possible, and after a while forget, or at least deny, that they ever had them at all.
>
> *Sermon 43, "The Scripture Way of Salvation," Works 6:44*

Time for Silent Reflection and Journaling

Blessing

> *Your faithful love lasts forever, LORD!*
> *Don't let go of what your hands have made.*
> *Psalm 138:8b*

Forgiveness

Prayer of Presence

Here am I, your loving creature,
offering all that I am
and hope to become to you,
my loving Creator.

Accept the gift I bring
and make it fruitful
as you keep me faithful,
for I am yours.

Scripture

One day when Jesus was teaching, Pharisees and legal experts
were sitting nearby. They had come from every village in
Galilee and Judea, and from Jerusalem. Now the power of
the Lord was with Jesus to heal. Some men were bringing a
man who was paralyzed, lying on a cot. They wanted to carry
him in and place him before Jesus, but they couldn't reach
him because of the crowd. So they took him up on the roof and

lowered him—cot and all—through the roof tiles into the crowded room in front of Jesus. When Jesus saw their faith, he said, "Friend, your sins are forgiven."

The legal experts and Pharisees began to mutter among themselves, "Who is this who insults God? Only God can forgive sins!"

Jesus recognized what they were discussing and responded, "Why do you fill your minds with these questions? Which is easier—to say, 'Your sins are forgiven,' or to say, 'Get up and walk'? But so that you will know that the Human One has authority on the earth to forgive sins" —Jesus now spoke to the man who was paralyzed, "I say to you, get up, take your cot, and go home." Right away, the man stood before them, picked up his cot, and went home, praising God.

All the people were beside themselves with wonder. Filled with awe, they glorified God, saying, "We've seen unimaginable things today."

Luke 5:17-26

First Wesley Reading

Here I found the peace I had long sought in vain; for I was assured my sins were forgiven. Not indeed all at once, but by degrees; not in one moment, nor in one hour. For I could not immediately believe that I was forgiven, because of the mistake I was then in concerning forgiveness. I saw not then, that the first promise to the children of God is, "Sin shall no more reign over you;" but thought I was to feel it in me no more from the time it was forgiven. Therefore, although I had the mastery over it, yet I often feared it was not forgiven, because it still stirred in me, and at sometimes thrust sore at me that I might fall: Because, though it did not reign, it did remain in me; and I was continually tempted, though not overcome.

Journal from August 12, 1738, Works *1:121*

Reflections

The Wesley brothers had no doubt about the reality of sin, but it took them some time to discover the reality of forgiveness. We should not be surprised that our experience is similar to theirs. The faith and confidence in God's ability and desire to forgive any sin was slow in coming; but gradually the light dawned. It is true, we are justified by grace through faith. Our hope for forgiveness does not depend on our merit but on Jesus Christ's merit. Forgiveness and salvation, as life itself, are pure gifts. Nothing we can do will earn our salvation or our forgiveness.

In a culture that applauds independence, self-reliance, and self-centeredness, it is difficult to admit that we are hopeless and helpless without the saving work of Christ within us. We often carry burdens of unresolved guilt and unforgiven sin, wondering why we miss the joy, assurance, confidence, and strength in God that others witness to.

The good news dawned on the Wesley brothers in the month of May 1738. Following his Aldersgate experience, John reports the change in his life this way:

In the evening I went very unwillingly to a society in Aldersgate Street where one was reading Luther's preface to the Epistle to the Romans. About a quarter before nine, while he was describing the change which God works in the heart through faith in Christ, I felt my heart strangely warmed. I felt I did trust in Christ, Christ alone for salvation: And an assurance was given me, that he had taken away my sins, even mine, and saved me from the law of sin and death

Journal from May 22-24, 1738, Works *1:103*

Carrying the baggage of unforgiven sin or the weight of our refusal to forgive others is a burden that can squeeze joy out of our lives. But the good news we proclaim is that the assurance of sins forgiven is a gift God is eager to give to us all. It is a message that we need to hear often and will as we listen to the Wesleys' witness.

Second Wesley Reading

"As we forgive them that trespass against us."—In these words our Lord clearly declares on what condition and in what degree or manner, we may look to be forgiven of God. All our trespasses and sins are forgiven us, *if* we forgive, and as we forgive, others. This is a point of the utmost importance. And our blessed Lord is so jealous lest at any time we should let it slip out of our thoughts, that he not only inserts it in the body of his prayer, but presently after repeats it twice over. "If," saith he, "ye forgive men their trespasses, your heavenly Father will also forgive you; But if ye forgive not men their trespasses, neither will your Father forgive your trespasses." (Verses 14, 15). Secondly, God forgives us *as* we forgive others. So that if any malice or bitterness, if any taint of unkindness or anger remains, if we do not clearly, fully, and from the heart, forgive all men their trespasses, we so far cut short the forgiveness of our own: God cannot clearly and fully forgive us: He may show us some degree of mercy; but we will not suffer him to blot out all our sins, and forgive all our iniquities.

Sermon 26, "Sermon on the Mount, Discourse 6," Works 5:340

Time for Silent Reflection and Journaling

Blessing

Have faith in God! … Therefore I say to you, whatever you pray and ask for, believe that you will receive it, and it will be so for you. And whenever you stand up to pray, if you have something against anyone, forgive so that your Father in heaven may forgive your wrongdoings.

Mark 11:22b, 24-25

Forgive Each Other

Therefore, as God's choice, holy and loved,
put on compassion, kindness, humility,
gentleness, and patience.
Be tolerant with each other and,
if someone has a complaint against anyone,
forgive each other.
As the Lord forgave you,
so also forgive each other.
And over all these things put on love,
which is the perfect bond of unity.

Colossians 3:12-14

Justifying Grace

Prayer of Presence

> So now you, LORD—
>> don't hold back any of your compassion from me.
>
> Let your loyal love and faithfulness always protect me....
>
> But let all those who seek you
>> celebrate and rejoice in you,
>
> Let those who love your salvation always say,
>> "The LORD is great!"
>
> But me? I'm weak and needy.
>> Let my LORD think of me.
>
> You are my help and my rescuer.
>> My God, don't wait any longer!
>
> Psalm 40:11, 16-17

Scripture

> At one time you were like a dead person because of the things
> you did wrong and your offenses against God. You used to live
> like people of this world. You followed the rule of a destructive
> spiritual power. This is the spirit of disobedience to God's will

that is now at work in persons whose lives are characterized by disobedience. At one time you were like those persons. All of you used to do whatever felt good and whatever you thought you wanted so that you were children headed for punishment just like everyone else.

However, God is rich in mercy. He brought us to life with Christ while we were dead as a result of those things that we did wrong. He did this because of the great love that he has for us. You are saved by God's grace! And God raised us up and seated us in the heavens with Christ Jesus. God did this to show future generations the greatness of his grace by the goodness that God has shown us in Christ Jesus.

You are saved by God's grace because of your faith. This salvation is God's gift. It's not something you possessed. It's not something you did that you can be proud of. Instead, we are God's accomplishment, created in Christ Jesus to do good things. God planned for these good things to be the way that we live our lives.

Ephesians 2:1-10

First Wesley Reading

Thus look unto Jesus! There is the Lamb of God, who taketh away thy sins! Plead thou no works, no righteousness of thine own! no humility, contrition, sincerity! In nowise. That were, in very deed, to deny the Lord that bought thee. No: Plead thou, singly, the blood of the covenant, the ransom paid for thy proud, stubborn, sinful soul. Who art thou, that now seest and feelest both thine inward and outward ungodliness? Thou art the man! I want thee for my Lord! I challenge *thee* for a child of God by faith! The Lord hath need of thee. Thou who feelest thou art just fit for hell, art just fit to advance his glory; the glory of his free grace, justifying the ungodly and him that worketh not. O come quickly! Believe in the Lord Jesus: and thou, even thou, art reconciled to God.

Sermon 5, "Justification by Faith," Works 5:64

Reflections

There seems to be a human tendency to try and justify ourselves. We like to compare ourselves to those whose lives, in our view, are less moral or faithful than our own. It is not uncommon to hear political leaders and little children alike blame others for their condition or actions. While deep within we know we are not "good enough," we nevertheless try to justify ourselves. John Wesley had every reason to follow this line of thought. Growing up in the Anglican tradition, he was taught, and early in his life believed, that the way to salvation was found in a high morality and an abundance of good works. After all, these were (and still are) expected marks of a Christian. But he soon learned that this was an inadequate foundation for Christian theology and for Christian life. If we were required to earn our way to God we were without hope. However, the remedy was offered for our sin and rebellion; that remedy was faith in God's grace that reached out to all with the offer of justification, reconciliation, and restoration.

In his sermon "Salvation by Faith," Wesley declared "This then is the salvation which is through faith; a salvation from sin, and the consequences of sin, both often expressed in the word *justification....*"

We can never justify ourselves, be reconciled to God, or earn our way to heaven on our own. But the marvelous good news is that God offers it all to us as gift. We are saved, in this world and the next, by grace through faith. We are justified, our loving relationship with God is restored, by God's action and not our own. The apostle Paul put it this way, "Wretched man that I am! Who will rescue me from this body of death? Thanks be to God through Jesus Christ our Lord." What can we do to earn our salvation? Nothing! And yet a natural response to God's gracious gift is to give thanks and to determine to walk in harmony with God and God's way.

Second Wesley Reading

> I showed at large, 1. That the Lord's Supper was ordained by God, to be a means of conveying to men either preventing, or justifying, or sanctifying grace, according to their several necessities. 2. That the persons for whom it was ordained, are all those who know and feel that they want the grace of God, either to restrain them from sin, or to show their sins forgiven, or to renew their souls in the image of God. 3. That inasmuch as we come to his table, not to give him any thing, but to receive whatsoever he pleases to give. And, 4. That no fitness is required at the time of communicating, but a sense of our state, of our utter sinfulness and helplessness; every one who knows he is fit for hell, being fit to come to Christ, in this as well as all other ways of his appointment.
>
> *Journal from June 28, 1740,* Works *1:280*

Time for Silent Reflection and Journaling

Blessing

May the God of peace,
who brought back the great shepherd of the sheep,
our Lord Jesus,
from the dead by the blood of the eternal covenant,
equip you with every good thing to do his will,
by developing in us what pleases him through Jesus Christ.
To him be the glory forever and always. Amen.

Hebrews 13:20-21

Practicing Our Faith

Practicing our faith in the world
requires our deepest resolve,
our greatest faith,
our unwavering trust, and
a very, very large measure
of God's grace.

Sanctifying Grace

Prayer of Presence

God,
Greater than anything I can imagine,
Holiness purer and more brilliant than light,
Mercy that forgives, redeems, and leads to righteousness,
Love that accepts and embraces me just as I am,
Grace that sustains and molds me into more than I am,
Promised presence that will never forsake or leave me alone,

I tremble in awe of such greatness and love;
I fall on my knees in gratitude and humility;
I yield my will to yours;
I declare that I am yours alone
and invite you to do with me what you will
As I walk in the light and life
of your unfailing presence.

Scripture

I'm no longer in the world, but they are in the world, even
as I'm coming to you. Holy Father, watch over them in your

name, the name you gave me, that they will be one just as we are one. When I was with them, I watched over them in your name, the name you gave to me, and I kept them safe. None of them were lost, except the one who was destined for destruction, so that scripture would be fulfilled. Now I'm coming to you and I say these things while I'm in the world so that they can share completely in my joy. I gave your word to them and the world hated them, because they don't belong to this world, just as I don't belong to this world. I'm not asking that you take them out of this world but that you keep them safe from the evil one. They don't belong to this world, just as I don't belong to this world. Make them holy in the truth; your word is truth. As you sent me into the world, so I have sent them into the world. I made myself holy on their behalf so that they also would be made holy in the truth.

John 17:11-19

First Wesley Reading

They speak of sanctification (or holiness) as if it were an outward thing; as if it consisted chiefly, if not wholly, in those two points, 1. The doing no harm; 2. The doing good (as it is called,) that is, the using the means of grace, and helping our neighbor. I believe it to be an inward thing, namely, the life of God in the soul of man; a participation of the divine nature; the mind that was in Christ; or, the renewal of our heart, after the image of Him that created us.

Journal from September 13, 1739, Works 1:225

Reflections

Can we be good on our own? Can we do good on our own? Can we live a life of goodness, holiness on our own? . . . John Wesley believed that it was impossible without the help of God. Salvation and sanctification are always out of reach without the action of God.

It is God's sanctifying grace at work within us that leads us to transformation. It is the inner life that must be transformed if the outer life is to be changed. The desire for this transformation, as the transformation itself, is God at work within us. Sanctifying grace does not relieve us of our responsibility to love God and neighbor. It does assure us that by God's grace we can practice what scripture teaches us as the greatest commandments of all.

Wesley believed that the new birth was more than forgiveness and assurance. It involved "going on to perfection," a journey that all were challenged to pursue and a journey that none could make on their own. The life of holiness was the goal for everyone and sanctifying grace provided the desire and capacity to pursue it daily.

No Christian should live with the weight of unforgiven sin and unresolved guilt. The assurance that we are forgiven, that we can begin again with a new page of life upon which to write our story, is the gift of God's justifying grace for all. But this is not the end of our relationship with God, the end of faith, or the end of our journey toward righteousness. Rather, it is the beginning of a quest for a life of goodness and holiness.

In our better moments all of us want to walk with Jesus Christ in faithful companionship. We know from experience that it is not easy to do in our complex and broken world. The temptations and opportunities to be less than like Christ surround us daily. However the grace to be more than we are is even closer. It is God's work of transformation within, and it is offered to everyone. Sanctifying grace is already at work within us. Our challenge is to cooperate with openness to God and by receiving the gift of sanctifying grace. It is this grace, coupled with our disciplined life, that leads to a life of peace, assurance, faithfulness, and usefulness. It is the grace that leads us on the journey toward Christian perfection.

Second Wesley Reading

> There is, likewise, great variety in the manner and time of God's bestowing his sanctifying grace, whereby he enables his children to give him their whole heart, which we can in no wise account for. We know not why he bestows this on some, even before they ask for it; (some unquestionable instances of which we have seen;) on some, after they had sought it but a few days: And yet permits other believers to wait for it, perhaps twenty, thirty, or forty years; nay, and others, till a few hours, or even minutes, before their spirits return to him. For the various circumstances also which attend the fulfilling of that great promise, "I will circumcise thy heart, to love the Lord thy God with all thy heart and with all thy soul." God undoubtedly has reasons; but those reasons are generally hid from the children of men.

Sermon 69, "The Imperfection of Human Knowledge," Works 6:349

Time for Silent Reflection and Journaling

Blessing

> *Light is planted like seed for the righteous person;*
> *joy too for those whose heart is right.*
> *Rejoice in the LORD, righteous ones!*
> *Give thanks to his holy name!*

Psalm 97:11-12

The Means of Grace

Prayer of Presence

Sustaining God,
in whom we find our identity and our life,
thank you for this time apart with you.
I offer to you all of my life that I am able to give.
Accept and make holy the gift of self I bring
and send me from this place renewed, refreshed,
and redirected for effective ministry in your name. **Amen.**

Scripture

By his divine power the Lord has given us everything we need
for life and godliness through the knowledge of the one who
called us by his own honor and glory. Through his honor and
glory he has given us his precious and wonderful promises, that
you may share the divine nature and escape from the world's
immorality that sinful craving produces.

This is why you must make every effort to add moral excellence
to your faith; and to moral excellence, knowledge; and to

*knowledge, self-control; and to self-control, endurance; and to
endurance, godliness; and to godliness, affection for others; and
to affection for others, love. If all these are yours and they are
growing in you, they'll keep you from becoming inactive and
unfruitful in the knowledge of our Lord Jesus Christ. Whoever
lacks these things is shortsighted and blind, forgetting that they
were cleansed from their past sins.*

2 Peter 1:3-9

First Wesley Reading

By means of grace I understand outward signs, words, or
actions ordained of God and appointed for this end…to
be the ordinary channels whereby he might convey to men
preventing, justifying and sanctifying grace.

Sermon 16, "The Means of Grace," Works 5:197

Reflections

The means of grace give access to God's active presence in the world.
They provide the pathway back to God for those who have wandered and
prevent us from wandering away in the first place. The means of grace are
given to us for our salvation, but they are gifts that we must use if we are to
enjoy the benefit.

If we were to ask Wesley why our relationship with God seems more
distant than what the book of Acts describes, he would likely ask us if we
are fully utilizing the means of grace. Do you want a more vital relationship
with God? Use the means of grace. Do you long for the assurance of sins
forgiven? Use the means of grace. Do you feel a great need for God's intervention in your life? Use the means of grace. Do you want to experience
growth in your Christian life? Use the means of grace.

Following Christ was not easy in Wesley's time and it is not easy in our time. But God has made available for us the means of grace that permit us to stay connected with the One for whom all things are possible. It is inconceivable that we should live a transformed life without tapping into the resources of God to do that transforming work within us. Thomas Langford says that "grace is the specific expression of God's nature and will, an incarnate and continuing presence."

Read the Bible, pray personally and corporately, fast, worship, receive the sacrament, and I believe you will discover a multitude of resources entering your life through the disciplined use of the means of grace. While we cannot force God to love us, redeem us, or sustain us, we can, through the means of grace, place ourselves in a position to receive God's great and good gifts each day.

Second Wesley Reading

Beware…of imagining you shall obtain the end without using the means conducive to it. God can give the end without any means at all; but you have no reason to think he will. Therefore constantly and carefully use all those means which he has appointed to be the ordinary channels of his grace. Use every means which either reason or Scripture recommends, as conducive (through the free love of God in Christ) either to the obtaining or increasing any of the gifts of God. Thus expect a daily growth in that pure and holy religion which the world always did, and always will, call enthusiasm:—but which, to all who are saved from real enthusiasm, from merely nominal Christianity, is "the wisdom of God and the power of God;" a glorious image of the Most High; "righteousness and peace;" a "fountain of living water, springing up into everlasting life!"

Sermon 37, "The Nature of Enthusiasm," Works 5:478

Time for Silent Reflection and Journaling

Blessing

Forgiven, free from sin, and the burdens of life, receive the peace of Christ for a restful and refreshing night, embraced in the everlasting arms of God.

Holiness of Life

Prayer of Presence

God revealed in so many ways
The beauty and magnificence of creation
The words of prophet, priest, and servant
The life, death, resurrection of Jesus
The power and constant presence of your Spirit
The witness of your servant saints and
Your sustaining grace that gives me life

I bring myself into your presence
Not to tell you what to do
But to invite you to be my honored guest
As I offer to you all that I am
All that I hope to become
And invite your transforming presence
To shape me more and more into your
Beloved and faithful child
For I am yours and I belong to you
My faithful Savior and Guide.

Scripture

So, brothers and sisters, because of God's mercies, I encourage you to present your bodies as a living sacrifice that is holy and pleasing to God. This is your appropriate priestly service. Don't be conformed to the patterns of this world, but be transformed by the renewing of your minds so that you can figure out what God's will is—what is good and pleasing and mature.

Because of the grace that God gave me, I can say to each one of you: don't think of yourself more highly than you ought to think. Instead, be reasonable since God has measured out a portion of faith to each one of you. We have many parts in one body, but the parts don't all have the same function. In the same way, though there are many of us, we are one body in Christ, and individually we belong to each other. We have different gifts that are consistent with God's grace that has been given to us.

Romans 12:1-6a

First Wesley Reading

St. Peter expresses it in a still different manner, though to the same effect: "As he that hath called you is holy, so be ye holy in all manner of conversation." (1 Peter 1:15.) According to this Apostle, then, perfection is another name for universal holiness: Inward and outward righteousness: Holiness of life, arising from holiness of heart.

Sermon 76, "On Perfection," Works 6:414

Reflections

Many assert that John Wesley was the world's most influential social reformer of his day. While some will question the depth of his influence, none question his remarkable ability to link piety with justice and to translate doctrine into daily living. From the early days at Oxford until a few days before his death, Wesley was about the ministry of caring for the poor, the oppressed, and the imprisoned. And all of this while living a rigorous life of prayer, study, and reflection.

Holy living is a direct result of and inseparable from a holy heart. To experience Christian perfection is to live as Jesus lived. It is to be obedient to the One proclaimed as Savior and Lord. Matthew 25 is a text to be taken seriously. To know Christ and to be known by Christ means to walk with Christ in the everyday business of life.

Certainly one of the goals of the societies, bands, and classes was to help people live the holy life. While each had some distinctive characteristics there was one common purpose. The meetings, the confessions, the prayers, the admonishment, the encouragement, the teaching were all designed to aid the participant in the translation of the gospel story into everyday living. To fail to practice holy living was to place in jeopardy one's relationship to God.

As early as the Oxford Holy Club days the spiritual quest for holiness centered in a pure heart and a transformed life.

This transformed life within led to a transformed life without. For the Wesleys the only reasonable response to God's grace and activity within was a faithful living out, an imitation of the One "who went about doing good." Obedience to Christ meant seeking to fashion all of life in keeping with the life of Jesus. Such obedience translated naturally into a life of holiness where love of God and love of neighbor were the guiding principle and the evident fruit of faith in the life of the believer.

Second Wesley Reading

By Methodists I mean, a people who profess to pursue (in whatsoever measure they have attained) holiness of heart and life, inward and outward conformity in all things to the revealed will of God; who place religion in an uniform resemblance of the great object of it; in a steady imitation of Him they worship, in all his imitable perfections; more particularly, in justice, mercy, and truth, or universal love filling the heart, and governing the life.

Advice to the People Called Methodists, Works *8:352*

Time for Silent Reflection and Journaling

Blessing

Happy are those who trust in the LORD,
  who rely on the LORD.
They will be like trees planted by the streams,
  whose roots reach down to the water.
They won't fear drought when it comes;
  their leaves will remain green.
They won't be stressed in the time of drought
  or fail to bear fruit.

Jeremiah 17:7-8

Opposition Along the Way

Prayer of Presence

> Establish justice for me, God!
> > Argue my case against ungodly people!
> > Rescue me from the dishonest and unjust!
> Because you are my God, my protective fortress!
> > Why have you rejected me?
> > Why do I have to walk around,
> > > sad, oppressed by enemies?
> Send your light and truth—those will guide me!
> > Let them bring me to your holy mountain,
> > > to your dwelling place.
> Let me come to God's altar—
> let me come to God, my joy, my delight—
> > then I will give you thanks with the lyre, God, my God!
>
> Why, I ask myself, are you so depressed?
> > Why are you so upset inside?
> > Hope in God!
> > > Because I will again give him thanks,
> > > my saving presence and my God.

Psalm 43

Scripture

"Look, I'm sending you as sheep among wolves. Therefore, be wise as snakes and innocent as doves. Watch out for people—because they will hand you over to councils and they will beat you in their synagogues. They will haul you in front of governors and even kings because of me so that you may give your testimony to them and to the Gentiles. Whenever they hand you over, don't worry about how to speak or what you will say, because what you can say will be given to you at that moment. You aren't doing the talking, but the Spirit of my Father is doing the talking through you....

"Disciples aren't greater than their teacher, and slaves aren't greater than their master. It's enough for disciples to be like their teacher and slaves like their master. If they have called the head of the house Beelzebul, it's certain that they will call the members of his household by even worse names."

Therefore, don't be afraid of those people because nothing is hidden that won't be revealed, and nothing secret that won't be brought out into the open. What I say to you in the darkness, tell in the light; and what you hear whispered, announce from the rooftops. Don't be afraid of those who kill the body but can't kill the soul. Instead, be afraid of the one who can destroy both body and soul in hell. Aren't two sparrows sold for a small coin? But not one of them will fall to the ground without your Father knowing about it already. Even the hairs of your head are all counted. Don't be afraid. You are worth more than many sparrows.

Matthew 10:16-20, 24-31

First Wesley Reading

I never saw before, no, not at Walsal itself, the hand of God so plainly shown as here. There I had many companions who were willing to die with me: Here, not a friend, but one simple girl, who likewise was hurried away from me in an instant, as soon as ever she came out of Mrs. B.'s door. There I received some blows, lost part of my clothes, and was covered over with dirt: Here, although the hands of perhaps some hundreds of people were lifted up to strike or throw, yet they were one and all stopped in the mid-way; so that not a man touched me with one of his fingers; neither was any thing thrown from first to last; so that I had not even a speck of dirt on my clothes. Who can deny that God heareth the prayer, or that he heareth the prayer, or that he hath all power in heaven and earth.

Journal from July 4, 1745, Works *1:505*

Reflections

A casual glimpse at the life of John Wesley may lead us to believe that life for him was without opposition. He knew where God was calling him to go, who God was calling him to be, and the rest was simple.

A deeper gaze at his life and ministry as revealed through his writing and the testimony of those who wrote about him suggests that he faced real opposition from the beginning until the end. Life was not simple or easy. The struggle for faithful discipleship resulted in opposition within his own life and opposition from those who could not agree with the way he had chosen. The search for authentic discipleship led him to go far beyond the common understanding or practice of Christian faith, and this going beyond the commonly accepted way often led to opposition.

His unrelenting commitment to personal and social holiness led him to an unpopular view of piety, riches, and responsibility for the poor. These convictions were rooted in his theology and nurtured by his experience. So opposition grew to his theology and his practice of that theology. Seeking to live out his faith, he was led to what appeared to be a radical response to the call to discipleship. Such a radical response sent shock waves through the Anglican Church and the culture and prompted external criticism and opposition.

There was also inner opposition. Wesley's journal reveals that he struggled for faith, questioned his own theology, was perplexed by his own journey toward perfection, and often felt that he had himself missed the mark and failed to practice what he preached.

The opposition he faced through all of life did not result in a gloomy attitude about life or the Christian faith.... He was able to see through the cross of life to the empty tomb. Opposition then became another gift from God to direct, form, and shape his journey of discipleship.

The powers of this world do not want to see their authority and control usurped by another, even if that other is God. To preach a message and practice a life of authentic discipleship will make us uncomfortable and make others anxious and sometimes hostile. We are not above the struggle of what it means to follow Jesus. The complex issues of life do not lend themselves to easy answers. It is not easy to know with certainty the path we are to follow. And often, after careful discernment, the direction we hear is not the way we would have chosen. There is often resistance within us to the way we are convinced God is calling us to travel. It is a strenuous journey of faith that permits us to say with Mary, "Here I am, the servant of the Lord; let it be with me according to your word" (Luke 1:38).

Second Wesley Reading

But about September, 1739, while my brother and I were absent, certain men crept in among them unawares, greatly troubling and subverting their souls; telling them, they were in a delusion, that they had deceived themselves, and had no true faith at all. "For," said they, "none has any justifying faith, who has ever any doubt or fear, which you know you have; or who has not a clean heart, which you know you have not: Nor will you ever have it, till you leave off using the means of grace; (so called;) till you leave off running to church and sacrament, and praying, and singing, and reading either the Bible, or any other book; for you cannot use these things without trusting in them. Therefore, till you leave them off, you can never have true faith; you can never till then trust in the blood of Christ."

Journal in Preface from February 1, 1737–8,
To His Return From Germany, Works *1:81*

Time for Silent Reflection and Journaling

Blessing

O God of Mercy, make yourself known to me. Illumine and remove from my life those sins and distractions that prevent me from being attentive and faithful. Grant to me faith, wisdom, and courage to see and rejoice in your promises for my future. **Amen.**

Following Jesus

To abandon the way of the world
and follow the way of Jesus
is a bold move and requires
honest, careful, and prayerful consideration.
It is not an inconsequential decision.

Saving Faith

Prayer of Presence

> I say to the LORD, "You are my refuge, my stronghold!
>   You are my God—the one I trust!"…
>
> God will protect you with his pinions;
>   you'll find refuge under his wings.
>   His faithfulness is a protective shield.
> Don't be afraid of terrors at night,
>   arrows that fly in daylight,
>   or sickness that prowls in the dark,
>   destruction that ravages at noontime.…
>
> Because he will order his messengers to help you,
>   to protect you wherever you go.
> They will carry you with their own hands
>   so you don't bruise your foot on a stone.
> You'll march on top of lions and vipers;
>   you'll trample young lions and serpents underfoot.

God says, "Because you are devoted to me,
  I'll rescue you.
  I'll protect you because you know my name.
Whenever you cry out to me, I'll answer.
  I'll be with you in troubling times.
  I'll save you and glorify you.
  I'll fill you full with old age.
  I'll show you my salvation."

Psalm 91:2, 4-6, 11-16

Scripture

May the God and Father of our Lord Jesus Christ be blessed! On account of his vast mercy, he has given us new birth. You have been born anew into a living hope through the resurrection of Jesus Christ from the dead. You have a pure and enduring inheritance that cannot perish—an inheritance that is presently kept safe in heaven for you. Through his faithfulness, you are guarded by God's power so that you can receive the salvation he is ready to reveal in the last time.

You now rejoice in this hope, even if it's necessary for you to be distressed for a short time by various trials. This is necessary so that your faith may be found genuine. (Your faith is more valuable than gold, which will be destroyed even though it is itself tested by fire.) Your genuine faith will result in praise, glory, and honor for you when Jesus Christ is revealed. Although you've never seen him, you love him. Even though you don't see him now, you trust him and so rejoice with a glorious joy that is too much for words. You are receiving the goal of your faith: your salvation.

1 Peter 1:3-9

First Wesley Reading

That great truth, "that we are saved by faith," will never be worn out; and that sanctifying as well as justifying faith is the free gift of God. Now, with God one day is as a thousand years. It plainly follows, that the quantity of time is nothing to Him: Centuries, years, months, days, hours, and moments are exactly the same. Consequently, he can as well sanctify in a day after we are justified, as a hundred years. There is no difference at all, unless we suppose Him to be such a one as ourselves.

Letter to Mrs. A. F., October 12, 1764, Works 12:333

Reflections

It is difficult to imagine God's unconditional love and grace that reach out to us and offer salvation without cost. It seems too good to be true. God's gracious offer of salvation in this world and the next, and our own faith, is all it takes to receive salvation? Hard to believe. And yet John Wesley, along with other giants of the church, proclaimed this message.

Salvation by faith means that no one is excluded from the Table of the Lord. The heavenly banquet is spread for all and none is prevented from participation. Social, political, financial, physical, and educational requirements often determine where we can gain entrance in this world; but not so in the Kingdom of God. Here, all are wanted and welcome. Here the only requirement is desire for the gift and faith to receive it.

Wesley was convinced that salvation was more than just being seated at the heavenly banquet, although it did include that. For him salvation encompassed all of life, including deliverance from the bondage of sin and enjoyment of the fruits of faithfulness in this life, as well as life in the world to come. For Wesley salvation was not of our doing but completely a gift from God. Without God's gracious call and generous offer we could never even respond. Salvation is a gift of God, initiated by God and completed by God. Even the faith to receive salvation is a gift.

Although faith is the only requirement for salvation, Wesley was convinced that saving faith had some consequences. These consequences could be observed and evaluated. Saving faith resulted in acts of mercy, compassion, devotion, and witness. While these acts were not requirements for salvation, they were signs of salvation. God works with the faithful to at once begin living within the Kingdom of God. Salvation means the incorporation of the ways of God into one's daily life as surely as it means forgiveness of sin and assurance of eternal reward.

Second Wesley Reading

> For by grace are ye saved through faith; and that not of yourselves. Of yourselves cometh neither your faith nor your salvation: It is the gift of God; the free, undeserved gift; the faith through which ye are saved, as well as the salvation, which he of his own good pleasure, his mere favour, annexes thereto. That ye believe, is one instance of his grace; that, believing, ye are saved, another. Not of works, lest any man should boast. For all our works, all our righteousness, which were before our believing, merited nothing of God but condemnation: So far were they from deserving faith, which therefore, whenever given, is not of works. Neither is salvation of the works we do when we believe: For it is then God that worketh in us: And, therefore, that he giveth us a

reward for what he himself worketh, only commendeth the riches of his mercy but leaveth us nothing whereof to glory.

Sermon 1, "Salvation by Faith," Works 5:13

Time for Silent Reflection and Journaling

Blessing

> *God is indeed my salvation;*
> *I will trust and won't be afraid.*
> *Yah, the LORD, is my strength and my shield;*
> *he has become my salvation.*
>
> *Isaiah 12:2*

Living Fully and Faithfully

Deep in the silence of our hearts,
we know we do want to follow Jesus.
We do know that following Jesus is the best
and only way for us to live fully and faithfully.
We really do know that it is the only way
to live a peaceful, joyful, fruitful life.

Do No Harm

Prayer of Presence

> Rescue me from evil people, LORD!
>> Guard me from violent people
>> who plot evil things in their hearts,
>> who pick fights every single day!
> They sharpen their tongues like a snake's;
>> spider poison is on their lips.   Selah
>
> Protect me from the power of the wicked, LORD!
>> Guard me from violent people
>> who plot to trip me up!
> Arrogant people have laid a trap for me with ropes.
>> They've spread out a net alongside the road.
>> They've set snares for me.   Selah
>
> I tell the LORD, "You are my God!
>> Listen to my request for mercy, LORD!"
>
> Psalm 140:1-6

Scripture

> The legal experts and Pharisees brought a woman caught
> in adultery. Placing her in the center of the group, they

said to Jesus, *"Teacher, this woman was caught in the act of committing adultery. In the Law, Moses commanded us to stone women like this. What do you say?" They said this to test him, because they wanted a reason to bring an accusation against him. Jesus bent down and wrote on the ground with his finger.*

They continued to question him, so he stood up and replied, "Whoever hasn't sinned should throw the first stone." Bending down again, he wrote on the ground. Those who heard him went away, one by one, beginning with the elders. Finally, only Jesus and the woman were left in the middle of the crowd.

Jesus stood up and said to her, "Woman, where are they? Is there no one to condemn you?"

She said, "No one, sir."

Jesus said, "Neither do I condemn you. Go, and from now on, don't sin anymore."

John 8:3-11

First Wesley Reading

It may be easily believed, he who had this love in his heart would work no evil to his neighbour [*sic*]. It was impossible for him, knowingly and designedly, to do harm to any man. He was at the greatest distance from cruelty and wrong, from any unjust or unkind action. With the same care did he "set a watch before his mouth, and keep the door of his lips," lest he should offend in tongue, either against justice, or against mercy or truth. He put away all lying, falsehood and fraud:

neither was guile found in his mouth. He spake evil of no
man nor did an unkind word ever come out of his lips.

Sermon 4, "Scriptural Christianity," Works *5:41*

Reflections

Can we trust God enough to follow the ways of the Spirit rather than
the ways of the world? If we choose to follow this way, will we be seen as
weak and at the mercy of others rather than as powerful and in control of
every situation? If we choose this way, will our position be eroded and our
point lost? The risk seems so great and often our fears speak so much louder
than our faith.

Is it possible to live in this complex and violent world *without* doing
harm? Are we supposed to turn the other cheek to those who distort the
truth by selective use of the facts of any given situation? Is it wise to do no
harm to those who seek to harm us, our future, or our reputation?...Is it
possible to speak the truth in love and gentleness when others seem to speak
partial truth in anger and hatred?

It is a challenging path to walk. Yet, even a casual reading of the gospel
suggests that Jesus taught and practiced a way of living that did no harm....
The good news is that it is possible to practice a way of living that is in
harmony with the life of Jesus and survive, even thrive, in a world like ours.
It is both a challenging and rewarding way to live; and each of us, with
God's help, can live such a life fully, faithfully, and joyfully.

Wesley said that to continue on the way of salvation, that is living in
harmony with God, we should begin "by doing no harm, by avoiding evil
of every kind, especially that which is most generally practiced" (*The Book of
Discipline of The United Methodist Church*, 2004, para. 103)

To do no harm means that I will be on guard so that all my actions and
even my silence will not add injury to another of God's children or to any

part of God's creation. As did John Wesley and those in the early Methodist movement before me, I too will determine every day that my life will always be invested in the effort to bring healing instead of hurt; wholeness instead of division; and harmony with the ways of Jesus rather than with the ways of the world.

Second Wesley Reading

> At Epworth in Lincolnshire, the town where I was born, a beggar came to a house in the market place, and begged a morsel of bread, saying she was very hungry. The master bid her begone.... She called at a second, and begged a little small beer, saying she was very thirsty. She had much the same answer. At a third door she begged a little water; saying she was very faint. But this man also was too conscientious to encourage common beggars. The boys, seeing a ragged creature turned from door to door, began to pelt her with snowballs. She looked up, lay down, and died! Would you wish to be the man who refused that poor wretch a morsel of bread or a cup of water?
>
> *Sermon 112, "The Rich Man and Lazarus," Works 7:150*

Time for Silent Reflection and Journaling

Blessing

> *I raise my eyes toward the mountains.*
> *Where will my help come from?*
> *My help comes from the LORD,*
> *the maker of heaven and earth.*
>
> *Psalm 121:1-2*

Do Good

Prayer of Presence

> Giver of every good and perfect gift,
>> once more I desire to offer myself
>> and my ministry to you.
> Accept the offering I make
>> and lead me in paths of righteousness, goodness, and truth.
> Guide my life and ministry
>> in the way of faithfulness and fruitfulness. **Amen.**

Scripture

> Love should be shown without pretending. Hate evil, and
> hold on to what is good. Love each other like the members of
> your family. Be the best at showing honor to each other. Don't
> hesitate to be enthusiastic—be on fire in the Spirit as you serve
> the Lord! Be happy in your hope, stand your ground when
> you're in trouble, and devote yourselves to prayer. Contribute
> to the needs of God's people, and welcome strangers into your
> home. Bless people who harass you—bless and don't curse
> them. Be happy with those who are happy, and cry with those

who are crying. Consider everyone as equal, and don't think
that you're better than anyone else. Instead, associate with
people who have no status. Don't think that you're so smart.
Don't pay back anyone for their evil actions with evil actions,
but show respect for what everyone else believes is good.

If possible, to the best of your ability, live at peace with all people.
Romans 12:9-18

First Wesley Reading

There is scarce any possible way of doing good for which here is not daily occasion.... Here are poor families to be relieved; Here are children to be educated: Here are workhouses, wherein both young and old gladly receive the word of exhortation: Here are prisons, and therein a complication of all human wants.

Journal from March 28, 1739, Works 1:181

Reflections

The words of Jesus and Wesley suggest that doing good is a universal command. That is, doing good is not limited to those like me or those who like me. Doing good is directed at everyone, even those who do not fit my category of "worthy" to receive any good that I or others can direct their way. This command is also universal in that no one is exempt from it.

Doing good, like doing no harm, is a proactive way of living. I do not need to wait to be asked to do some good deed or provide some needed help. I do not need to wait until circumstances cry out for aid to relieve suffering or correct some horrible injustice. I can decide that my way of living will come down on the side of doing good to all in every circumstance and in every way I can. I can decide that I will choose a way of living that nourishes goodness and strengthens community.

This way of living will require a careful and continual assessment of my life and the world in which I live. It will require an even more bold and radical step than not doing harm to those who may disagree with me and even seek to harm me. For now I am committing myself to seeking good for everyone in God's world. Even those little offenses, like cutting in ahead of me in traffic, to the large offenses, such as considering me less than a child of God, can never move me outside the circle of goodness that flows from God to me and through me to the world. Every act and every word must pass through the love and will of God and there be measured to discover if its purpose does indeed bring good and goodness to all it touches.

Second Wesley Reading

> This commandment is written in his heart, "That he who loveth God, love his brother also." And he accordingly loves his neighbour [sic] as himself; he loves every man as his own soul. His heart is full of love to all mankind.... For he "loves his enemies;" yea, and the enemies of God, "the evil and unthankful." And if it be not in his power to "do good to them that hate him," yet he ceases not to pray for them.
>
> *The Character of a Methodist*, Works 8:343

Time for Silent Reflection and Journaling

Blessing

> The LORD is merciful and compassionate,
> very patient, and full of faithful love.
> The LORD is good to everyone and everything;
> God's compassion extends, to all his handiwork!
>
> Psalm 145:8-9

Stay in Love with God

Prayer of Presence

Loving Teacher,
Help us to open our minds, hearts,
and entire lives to you.
Come, speak to us,
Teach us,
Lead us,
and form us
until we are more and more like you
For we are yours.

Scripture

"I am the true vine, and my Father is the vineyard keeper. He removes any of my branches that don't produce fruit, and he trims any branch that produces fruit so that it will produce even more fruit. You are already trimmed because of the word I have spoken to you. Remain in me, and I will remain in you. A branch can't produce fruit by itself, but must remain in the vine. Likewise, you can't produce fruit unless you remain in

me. I am the vine; you are the branches. If you remain in me and I in you, then you will produce much fruit. Without me, you can't do anything. If you don't remain in me, you will be like a branch that is thrown out and dries up. Those branches are gathered up, thrown into a fire, and burned. If you remain in me and my words remain in you, ask for whatever you want and it will be done for you. My Father is glorified when you produce much fruit and in this way prove that you are my disciples."

John 15:1-8

First Wesley Reading

Beware…of imagining you shall obtain the end without using the means conducive to it. God can give the end without any means at all; but you have no reason to think he will. Therefore constantly and carefully use all those means which he has appointed to be the ordinary channels of his grace. Use every means which either reason or Scripture recommends, as conducive (through the free love of God in Christ) either to the obtaining or increasing any of the gifts of God. Thus expect a daily growth in that pure and holy religion which the world always did, and always will, call enthusiasm:—but which, to all who are saved from real enthusiasm, from merely nominal Christianity, is "the wisdom of God and the power of God;" a glorious image of the Most High; "righteousness and peace," a "fountain of living water, springing up into everlasting life!"

Sermon 37, "The Nature of Enthusiasm," Works 5:478

Reflections

Ordinance is a strange word to our ears. But to John Wesley, it was a word that described the practices that kept the relationship between God and humans vital, alive, and growing. He names public worship of God, The Lord's Supper, private and family prayer, searching the Scriptures, Bible study, and fasting as essential to a faithful life.... These practices can become a life-giving source of strength and guidance for us. Wesley saw these disciplines as central to any life of faithfulness to God in Christ. He saw that the consistent practice of these spiritual disciplines kept those who sought to follow Christ in touch with the presence and power of Christ so they could fulfill their desire to live as faithful disciples.

Spiritual disciplines teach us to live our lives in harmony with something larger than ourselves and larger than that which the world values as ultimate....

We may name our spiritual disciplines differently, but we too must find our way of living and practicing those disciplines that will keep us in love with God—practices that will help keep us positioned in such a way that we may hear and be responsive to God's slightest whisper of direction and receive God's promised presence and power every day and in every situation. It is in these practices that we learn to trust God as revealed in Jesus Christ. It is in these practices that we learn of God's love for us. It is where our love for God is nurtured and sustained. Incorporating these practices in our way of living will keep us in love with God and assure us of God's love for us in the world and the world to come.

When we say yes to God's call of love, we are released from so many things; and our freedom in Christ is a wonderful gift to be enjoyed. But we too will likely be led to places we had not intended to go. Disciples of Jesus do have great freedom in Christ, and they also have great loyalty to the way of Christ. Consequently, they are often called to action and restraint as they stay in love with God and seek to live a life of faithfulness, fidelity, and integrity.

Second Wesley Reading

> Keep close, I beseech you, to every means of grace. Strive to walk in all the ordinances and commandments of God blameless.... "Add to your faith virtue; to virtue knowledge; to knowledge temperance; to temperance patience; to patience godliness; to godliness...kindness; to...kindness charity."
>
> *Journal from April 1, 1762,* Works *3:88*

Time for Silent Reflection and Journaling

Blessing

> *Love the* LORD *your God with all your heart, all your being, and all your strength.*
>
> *Deuteronomy 6:5*

Life of God in the Soul

Prayer of Presence

Tender Shepherd,
Bring to my awareness your constant companionship,
To my weariness your matchless strength,
To my brokenness your healing touch,
And to my joy your blessing. **Amen**.

Scripture

"If you love me, you will keep my commandments. I will ask
the Father, and he will send another Companion, who will
be with you forever. This Companion is the Spirit of Truth,
whom the world can't receive because it neither sees him nor
recognizes him. You know him, because he lives with you and
will be with you.

"I won't leave you as orphans. I will come to you. Soon the
world will no longer see me, but you will see me. Because I
live, you will live too. On that day you will know that I am in
my Father, you are in me, and I am in you. Whoever has my

commandments and keeps them loves me. Whoever loves me
will be loved by my Father, and I will love them and reveal
myself to them. . . ."

Jesus answered, "Whoever loves me will keep my word. My
Father will love them, and we will come to them and make
our home with them."

John 14:15-21, 23

First Wesley Reading

Yet, on the authority of God's word, and our own Church,
I must repeat the question, "Hast thou received the Holy
Ghost?" If thou hast not, thou art not yet a Christian. For
a Christian is a man that is "anointed with the Holy Ghost
and with power." Thou art not yet made a partaker of pure
religion and undefiled. Dost thou know what religion is? that
it is a participation of the divine nature; the life of God in
the soul of man; Christ formed in the heart; "Christ in thee,
the hope of glory?" happiness and holiness; heaven begun on
earth? "a kingdom of God within thee; not meat and drink,"
no outward thing; "but righteousness, and peace, and joy
in the Holy Ghost?" and everlasting kingdom brought into
thy soul.

Sermon 3, "Awake, Thou that Sleepest," Works 5:30

Reflections

Charles Wesley captured [a] central theme of Wesleyan theology in
his hymn, "Love Divine, All Loves Excelling" (*UMH*, 384). Notice the
breadth and depth of thought and feeling in these few lines:

> Love divine, all loves excelling,
> joy of heaven, to earth come down;
> fix in us thy humble dwelling,
> all thy faithful mercies crown!
> Jesus, thou art all compassion,
> pure, unbounded love thou art;
> visit us with thy salvation;
> enter every trembling heart.

It was this divine love, pure and unbounded, that brought to John Wesley assurance of his own salvation and energized him to share this good news with the world. It was clear to Wesley that our lives, our faith, our salvation, our spiritual journey are all rooted in this unbounded and unconditional love of God.

Having experienced this unearned, undeserved, and unlimited love, it is not surprising that there was awakened in Wesley's heart a burning fire of love for God and for neighbor. The law of duty was consumed by the law and fire of love. Actions were no longer driven by fear but were inspired, fueled, and directed by the law of love.

It was this experience of God's love for him and an awakened love for God that firmly anchored Wesley's life in the spiritual disciplines that included acts of mercy and compassion as clearly as they included acts of piety and devotion.

Therefore it is not surprising that Wesley practiced and encouraged others to practice a way of life that expressed its faith in visible and real ways.

Second Wesley Reading

> His judgment concerning holiness is new. He no longer judges it to be an outward thing: To consist either in doing

no harm, in doing good, or in using the ordinances of God. He sees it is the life of God in the soul; the image of God fresh stamped on the heart; and entire renewal of the mind in every temper and thought, after the likeness of Him that created it.

Journal from October 6, 1738, Works 1:161

Time for Silent Reflection and Journaling

Blessing

May the God of peace and love dwell within us, accompany us, guide us, and keep us throughout the day and always. **Amen.**

When All I Hear Is Silence

Prayer of Presence

Grant to me, O God, the continual guidance, strength,
> and help of your Holy Spirit so that I may serve faithfully
> in your church and world.
Defend and uphold me and grant me grace
> to live in such a way as to please you
> and reflect your presence to others.
Hear and accept my prayer as I offer it and my life to you
> in gratitude for your steadfast love.
In the name of Christ. **Amen.**

Scripture

LORD, God of my salvation,
> by day I cry out,
> even at night, before you—
> let my prayer reach you!
Turn your ear to my outcry
> because my whole being is filled with distress;
> my life is at the very brink of hell.

I am considered as one of those plummeting into the pit.
I am like those who are beyond help,
drifting among the dead, lying in the grave, like dead bodies—
those you don't remember anymore,
those who are cut off from your power.
You placed me down in the deepest pit,
in places dark and deep.
Your anger smothers me;
you subdue me with it, wave after wave. Selah
You've made my friends distant.
You've made me disgusting to them.
I can't escape. I'm trapped!
My eyes are tired of looking at my suffering.
I've been calling out to you every day, LORD—
I've had my hands outstretched to you . . . !

But I cry out to you, LORD!
My prayer meets you first thing in the morning!
Why do you reject my very being, LORD?
Why do you hide your face from me?

Psalm 88:1-9, 13-14

First Wesley Reading

"I cannot find in myself the love of God, or of Christ…I have not that joy in the Holy Ghost; no settled, lasting joy. Nor have I such a peace as excludes the possibility either of fear or doubt. When holy men have told me I had no faith, I have often doubted whether I had or no."

Journal from October 14, 1738, Works 1:162

Reflections

While our hunger for God is universal and has been identified from the time of Adam and Eve as to be our own, those peak moments of communion or union with God are extremely rare. They are there, perhaps to lure us or to reassure us, but they are not there on command or with predictable regularity.... The plains of daily existence may be marked with deep awareness on the presence of another One who is near and who sustains, or the quiet companionship of One who guides and upholds, but there is awareness of a relationship that is life-giving.

Just as there are those peak moments of transcendence, however, there also seem to be those moments of night and silence when there is no voice of companionship and no light for our path. I say *seem to be* because theologically and rationally we declare that God is always with us. It is a truth central to our faith. In spite of the testimony of our faith and tradition, and even in the face of our theology and rational declaration of God's presence with us, in spite of all this, there are times when the reality we experience is a reality of absence, of night, and of silence.

Wesley's journal reveals that he struggled for faith, questioned his own theology, was perplexed by his own journey toward perfection, and often felt that he had himself missed the mark and failed to practice what he preached.

Standing in the silence we do not need to be convinced of its reality. But we do need to be reminded of another reality. Others have travelled this way before us and their testimony, plus the memories of our own experience with our faithful Savior up to this point, assures us that we are not alone. We are given signs and songs even in the darkest night, signs and songs that assure of the presence of the only One who can shatter our silence.

What will emerge on the other side of silence may not be clear, but there is ample evidence that we will emerge more whole and complete than when we entered. The silence, then, is not to be feared, but embraced, for it too will pass through the strong, competent, and gentle hands of our Savior, Jesus Christ. Once we stand on the other side of this experience, we will say with the author of Romans that nothing "in all creation will be able to separate us from the love of God in Christ Jesus our Lord" (Romans 8:39).

Second Wesley Reading

> The First I shall mention, as being more especially grievous to the Holy Spirit, is inconsiderateness and inadvertence to his holy motions within us. There is a particular frame and temper of soul, a sobriety of mind, with which the Spirit of God will not concur in the purifying of our hearts. It is in our power, through his preventing and assisting grace, to prepare this in ourselves; and he expects we should, this being the foundation of all his after-works. Now this consists in preserving our minds in a cool and serious disposition, in regulating and calming our affections, and calling in and checking the inordinate pursuits of our passions after the vanities and pleasures of this world; the doing of which is of such importance, that the very reason why men profit so little under the most powerful means, is, that they do not look enough within themselves,—they do not observe and watch the discords and imperfections of their own spirits, nor attend with care to the directions and remedies which the Holy Spirit is always ready to suggest.
>
> *Sermon 138, "On Grieving the Holy Spirit," Works 7:489*

Time for Silent Reflection and Journaling

Blessing

Open your hand to receive the gift of God's companionship anew. In abandonment, silence and darkness become almost insignificant and more and more of life is trusted to God.

Following Jesus

To follow Jesus is to follow a God
made known in Scripture, history, nature,
our innermost self, and—most of all—
in the life, death, and resurrection
of Jesus of Nazareth.
To follow Jesus is to follow One
who fully trusts in God's goodness, love,
and intimate involvement
in the affairs of humankind.
To follow this Jesus is to desire
to be like him in our living and our dying.

Searching the Scriptures

Prayer of Presence

I have sought you with all my heart.
> Don't let me stray from any of your commandments!
I keep your word close, in my heart,
> so that I won't sin against you.
You, LORD, are to be blessed!
> Teach me your statutes.
I will declare out loud
> all the rules you have spoken.
I rejoice in the content of your laws
> as if I were rejoicing over great wealth.
I will think about your precepts
> and examine all your paths.
I will delight in your statutes;
> I will not forget what you have said.

Psalm 119:10-16

Scripture

On that same day, two disciples were traveling to a village
called Emmaus, about seven miles from Jerusalem. They were
talking to each other about everything that had happened.
While they were discussing these things, Jesus himself arrived

and joined them on their journey. They were prevented from recognizing him.

He said to them, "What are you talking about as you walk along?" They stopped, their faces downcast.

The one named Cleopas replied, "Are you the only visitor to Jerusalem who is unaware of the things that have taken place there over the last few days?"

He said to them, "What things?"

They said to him, "The things about Jesus of Nazareth. Because of his powerful deeds and words, he was recognized by God and all the people as a prophet. But our chief priests and our leaders handed him over to be sentenced to death, and they crucified him. We had hoped he was the one who would redeem Israel. All these things happened three days ago. But there's more: Some women from our group have left us stunned. They went to the tomb early this morning and didn't find his body. They came to us saying that they had even seen a vision of angels who told them he is alive. Some of those who were with us went to the tomb and found things just as the women said. They didn't see him."

Then Jesus said to them, "You foolish people! Your dull minds keep you from believing all that the prophets talked about. Wasn't it necessary for the Christ to suffer these things and then enter into his glory?" Then he interpreted for them the things written about himself in all the scriptures, starting with Moses and going through all the Prophets.

Luke 24:13-27

First Wesley Reading

I showed, concerning the Holy Scriptures, 1. That to search (that is, read and hear them,) is a command of God. 2. That this command is given to all, believers and unbelievers. 3. That this is commanded or ordained as a means of grace, a means of conveying the grace of God to all, whether unbelievers (such as to whom faith cometh by hearing) or believers, who by experience know, that "all Scripture is profitable," or a means to this end, "that the man of God may be perfect, thoroughly furnished to all good works."

Journal from June 26, 1740, Works *1:279*

Reflections

The Bible continues to be a best seller, and it is prominently displayed in the hands or under the arm of prominent people.... The perplexing social issues of our time often become the battleground for competing understandings and a variety of uses and misuses of the Bible. Each side can find justification for its position and ammunition to destroy its opponents' position....

John Wesley was a competent biblical scholar, reading the Bible in the original languages, and was well trained at Oxford and as a priest in the Church of England. However, he never placed himself above the scripture. He was fearless in his scholarship and yet utterly obedient to the scripture's message for his ministry and for all of life.

Wesley knew that the transformed life was not accidental. He was convinced that one does not drift into inward or outward holiness. God's grace required response and that response included a careful reading, reflection upon, and incorporation of and obedience to scripture in everyday living. God's grace was always available and scripture was one way for Christians to appropriate that grace into daily life.

Do you wish to live a life of inward and outward holiness? Do you desire to live with God in the midst of this broken world? Do you desire some guiding principles that can bring direction to your personal and corporate decision-making? If the answer is yes to any of these questions, you will want to read and reflect upon the scriptures. For scripture remains the primary source of revelation and authority for those who are descendants of Wesley....

In an age of accelerated change and great uncertainty most of us look for some authority or guiding principle that will not only help us understand what is happening in the world, but will help us to live peacefully, fruitfully, and faithfully as Christians. The scriptures, carefully, prayerfully, and honestly read, can provide that vast resource of wisdom and direction for us.

Second Wesley Reading

> Would it not be advisable, (1.) To set apart a little time, if you can, every morning and evening for that purpose? (2.) At each time, if you have leisure, to read a chapter out of the Old, and one out of the New, Testament; if you cannot do this, to take a single chapter or a part of one? (3.) To read this with a single eye, to know the whole will of God, and a fixed resolution to do it?
>
> *Works Abridged from Various Authors,* Works *14:253*

Time for Silent Reflection and Journaling

Blessing

> *The LORD counsels those who honor him;*
> *he makes his covenant known to them.*
>
> *Psalm 25:14*

Prayer

Prayer of Presence

> Lord, you have examined me.
>> You know me....
>
> Where could I go to get away from your spirit?
>> Where could I go to escape your presence?
> If I went up to heaven, you would be there.
>> If I went down to the grave, you would be there too!
> If I could fly on the wings of dawn,
>> stopping to rest only on the far side of the ocean—
>>> even there your hand would guide me;
>>> even there your strong hand would hold me tight!
> If I said, "The darkness will definitely hide me;
>> the light will become night around me,"
>> even then the darkness isn't too dark for you!
>>> Nighttime would shine bright as day,
>>> because darkness is the same as light to you!...
>
> God, your plans are incomprehensible to me!
>> Their total number is countless!

If I tried to count them—they outnumber grains of sand!
   If I came to the very end—I'd still be with you....

Examine me God! Look at my heart!

Psalm 139:1, 7-12, 17-18, 23

Scripture

Jesus was praying in a certain place. When he finished, one of his disciples said, "Lord, teach us to pray, just as John taught his disciples."

Jesus told them, "When you pray, say:

   'Father, uphold the holiness of your name.
   Bring in your kingdom.
   Give us the bread we need for today.
   Forgive us our sins,
      for we also forgive everyone who has wronged us.
   And don't lead us into temptation.'"

He also said to them, "Imagine that one of you has a friend and you go to that friend in the middle of the night. Imagine saying, 'Friend, loan me three loaves of bread because a friend of mine on a journey has arrived and I have nothing to set before him.' Imagine further that he answers from within the house, 'Don't bother me. The door is already locked, and my children and I are in bed. I can't get up to give you anything.' I assure you, even if he wouldn't get up and help because of his friendship, he will get up and give his friend whatever he needs because of his friend's brashness. And I tell you: Ask and you will receive. *Seek and you will find. Knock and the door will be opened to you. Everyone who asks, receives. Whoever seeks, finds. To everyone who knocks, the door is opened.*

Luke 11:1-10

First Wesley Reading

"But what good works are those, the practice of which you affirm to be necessary to sanctification?" First, all works of piety; such as public prayer, family prayer, and praying in our closet; receiving the supper of the Lord; searching the Scriptures, by hearing, reading, meditating; and using such a measure of fasting or abstinence as our bodily health allows.

Sermon 43, "The Scripture Way of Salvation," Works *6:51*

Reflections

Prayer is a natural part of our human experience. All of us pray. Sometimes we pray only when we are at the peak of our powers and simply must thank someone; and sometimes we pray when we are at the very depth of despair and we simply cry out to God in our agony. Both of these times of prayer are natural and appropriate. But they are not enough to sustain us or to nurture our relationship with God.

Therefore we, as Wesley before us, Luther before him, Augustine before him, and Jesus before them all, need to establish a disciplined life of prayer. Since each of us is a unique creation of God, our life of prayer will be unique as well. We may each pray at different times, use different resources, pray for different lengths of time, pray more in solitude or pray more in community. It is important to recognize our differences as we fashion our way of living prayerfully.

When we read Wesley's journal and reflect upon his disciplined life, we can easily be convinced that such a life or prayer is impossible in our time and our situation. Life is more complex and is changing more rapidly now than in the eighteenth century. The pressures on our time and life are different and more varied than the pressures John Wesley experienced. On the other hand, this kind of reflection on Wesley's life makes it clear that he often lived in a time squeeze and felt himself to be in a pressure cooker just as we do. Looking back over two centuries it is easy to see that this pressure cooker was, for the most part, self imposed and fueled by his sense of mission. He was able to live creatively within this pressure because he continued a disciplined life of prayer.

Prayer is God's greatest provision for our spiritual life. Our relationship with God is impossible without prayer. We cannot know God's mind or heart without prayer. We cannot receive God's direction, hear God's voice, or respond to God's call without prayer. Since this is true, prayer is also God's greatest provision for all of life. It is the supreme means of grace given to all humankind.

Second Wesley Reading

> For indeed [a Methodist] "prays without ceasing." It is given him "always to pray and not to faint." Not that he is always in the house of prayer; though he neglects no opportunity of being there. Neither is he always on his knees, although he often is, or on his face, before the Lord his God. Nor yet is he always crying aloud to God, or calling upon him in words: For many times "the Spirit maketh intercession for him with groans that cannot be uttered.…"

And while he thus always exercises his love to God, by praying without ceasing, rejoicing evermore, and in everything giving thanks, this commandment is written in his heart, "That he who loveth God, love his brother also." And he accordingly loves his neighbor as himself; he loves every man as his own soul.

The Character of a Methodist, Works *8:343*

Time for Silent Reflection and Journaling

Blessing

Creator of all that exists and lover of all you have made,
Bless me with eyes to see your presence in the world you love,
Ears to hear your tender voice of guidance,
And courage to say, "Here I am, use me this day
for I am yours."

Prayer Is a Way of Living

Prayer at its best is
not an additive to life;
rather it is a way of living.
It was so for Jesus and
it may be so for us.

The Lord's Supper

Prayer of Presence

Merciful God,
we confess that we have not loved you with our whole heart.
We have failed to be an obedient church.
We have not done your will,
we have broken your law,
we have rebelled against your love,
we have not loved our neighbors,
and we have not heard the cry of the needy.
Forgive us, we pray,
Free us for joyful obedience,
through Jesus Christ our Lord. **Amen**.

Scripture

Jesus told them, "I assure you, it wasn't Moses who gave the
bread from heaven to you, but my Father gives you the true
bread from heaven. The bread of God is the one who comes
down from heaven and gives life to the world."

They said, "Sir, give us this bread all the time!"

Jesus replied, "I am the bread of life. Whoever comes to me
will never go hungry, and whoever believes in me will never
be thirsty. But I told you that you have seen me and still don't
believe. Everyone whom the Father gives to me will come to
me, and I won't send away anyone who comes to me. I have
come down from heaven not to do my will, but the will of him
who sent me. This is the will of the one who sent me, that I
won't lose anything he has given me, but I will raise it up at
the last day. This is my Father's will: that all who see the Son
and believe in him will have eternal life, and I will raise them
up at the last day."

John 6:32-40

First Wesley Reading

We allow likewise, that all outward means whatever, if separate from the Spirit of God, cannot profit at all, cannot conduce, in any degree, either to the knowledge or love of God. Without controversy, the help that is done upon earth, He doeth it himself. It is He alone who, by his own almighty power, worketh in us what is pleasing in his sight; and all outward things, unless He work in them and by them, are mere weak and beggarly elements. Whosoever, therefore, imagines there is any intrinsic power in any means whatsoever, does greatly err, not knowing the Scriptures, neither the power of God. We know that there is no inherent power in the words that are spoken in prayer, in the letter of the Scripture read, the sound thereof heard, or the bread and wine received in the Lord's Supper; but that it is God alone who is the Giver of every good gift, the Author of all grace; that the whole power is of Him, whereby, through any of these, there is any blessing conveyed to our souls.

Sermon 16, "The Means of Grace,"Works 5:188

Reflections

There are many places where each one of us is excluded. The Table of the Lord is one place where all are included. Everyone is invited and welcomed to this table. Our social structure is often built on distinction that gives and takes power. The Lord's Supper is built on our oneness with Christ and with one another. At this table power flows equally to all; none is excluded, and none need go away empty.

Here we speak not of what we have accomplished, but of what God has accomplished through the life, death, and resurrection of Jesus Christ. At this table we are reconciled to God, to neighbor, and even within ourselves. Here we are all offered the gifts of God's redemption and peace, gifts that we have not earned and never can earn in the future. Here we are offered the incomprehensible, communion with God. At this table our hunger for God can be satisfied, our yearning for holiness directed, our purpose for life clarified, and our vision of the meaning of life made clear.

Because all of this is true, the Lord's Supper is a remarkable sign of the reign of God. Here we have a glimpse into what God intends for all humanity. And yet we confess that God's intention is often far from the reality we experience. Unfortunately, even the Lord's Table can be profaned....

At the Lord's Table there is enough for all. No matter how broken, hungry, or needy I am, there is always enough of the bread of life for me. And my need does not prevent another's need from being recognized and met. No one is shortchanged or denied what is needed. My great need does not jeopardize the resources for my sister or brother. At the Lord's Table there is enough for all....

It is not surprising that Wesley encouraged people to take Communion at least once every week and that he received this gift for himself with even greater frequency. It was for him a constant source of nourishment, healing, and direction.

Second Wesley Reading

> Many were comforted and strengthened both at the Lord's Supper, and at the evening service. I think all jealousies and misunderstandings are now vanished, and the whole society is well knit together. How long will they continue so, considering the unparalleled fickleness of the people in these parts? That God knows. However, he does work now and we rejoice therein.
>
> *Journal from February 1, 1761,* Works *3:39*

Time for Silent Reflection and Journaling

Blessing

Hear the good news:
    Christ died for us while we were yet sinners;
    That proves God's love toward us.
In the name of Jesus Christ, you are forgiven.

Reaching Out to the Poor

Prayer of Presence

> With all my heart I glorify the Lord!
>> In the depths of who I am I rejoice in God my savior.
> He has looked with favor on the low status of his servant.
>> Look! From now on, everyone will consider me highly
>> favored
>>> because the mighty one has done great things for me.
> Holy is his name.
>> He shows mercy to everyone,
>>> from one generation to the next,
>>> who honors him as God.
> He has shown strength with his arm.
>> He has scattered those with arrogant thoughts and proud
>> inclinations.
> He has pulled the powerful down from their thrones
>> and lifted up the lowly.
> He has filled the hungry with good things
>> and sent the rich away empty-handed.

Luke 1:46b-53

Scripture

Brothers and sisters, we want to let you know about the grace of God that was given to the churches of Macedonia. While they were being tested by many problems, their extra amount of happiness and their extreme poverty resulted in a surplus of rich generosity. I assure you that they gave what they could afford and even more than they could afford, and they did it voluntarily. . . .

I'm not giving an order, but by mentioning the commitment of others, I'm trying to prove the authenticity of your love also. You know the grace of our Lord Jesus Christ. Although he was rich, he became poor for our sakes, so that you could become rich through his poverty.

I'm giving you my opinion about this. It's to your advantage to do this, since you not only started to do it last year but you wanted to do it too. Now finish the job as well so that you finish it with as much enthusiasm as you started, given what you can afford. A gift is appreciated because of what a person can afford, not because of what that person can't afford, if it's apparent that it's done willingly. It isn't that we want others to have financial ease and you financial difficulties, but it's a matter of equality. At the present moment, your surplus can fill their deficit so that in the future their surplus can fill your deficit. In this way there is equality. As it is written, The one who gathered more didn't have too much, and the one who gathered less didn't have too little.

2 Corinthians 8:1-3, 8-15

First Wesley Reading

> Dear Sir, I know what you feel for the poor, and I also sympathize with you. Here is a hard season coming on, and everything very dear; thousands of pour souls, yea, Christians dread the approaching calamities. O that God would stir up the hearts of all that believe themselves his children, to evidence it by showing mercy to the poor, as God has shown them mercy! Surely the real children of God will do it of themselves; for it is the natural fruit of a branch in Christ. I would not desire them to lose one meal in a week, but to use as cheap food, clothes... as possible.
>
> *Journal from November 20, 1767, Works 3:307*

Reflections

One of the few things John Wesley feared was the accumulation of wealth. As a biblical scholar and a practical theologian he was convinced that to follow Jesus Christ meant involvement with, and ministry among and to, the poor....

This understanding of the relationship between following Christ and involvement with the poor led him to some unusual practices....

His journal is filled with entries that describe his experiences of visiting the poor, the prisoner, the sorrowing and the suffering. The false stereotypes of the day were shattered as he came to work with and to know the poor and needy of the world. Had he ignored God's urging to ministry with the poor he would have missed a large segment of the population that turned toward Christ through the Methodist movement. He would also have missed living and witnessing to a balanced faith that emphasized love for God and love for neighbor in very simple and practical ways....

Gifted scholar and preacher that he was, John Wesley could have ignored the poor and had a fruitful ministry with persons in the middle and upper middle class. But he chose to relate to all, especially those with special needs. Prisoners, the sick, orphans, widows, the poor, and all who suffered received his care because he believed them to be special recipients of God's care. He was certain that if God was God of all, then no follower of God could turn away from the pain, suffering, or need of any of God's children....

In a world where the chasm between rich and poor is growing at an alarming rate, the Methodist model is both promising and threatening. It is promising in that here is an answer to the incredible suffering of the poor in our land and around the world. It is threatening because no one can escape responsibility for the needs of another. In Wesley's view we are our brothers' keeper, and as long as there is one person in need, no Christian can rest content.

Second Wesley Reading

> He [John Fletcher] frequently said he was never happier than when he had given away the last penny he had in his house. If at any time I had gold in my drawers, it seemed to afford him no comfort. But if he could find a handful of small silver, when he was going out to see the sick, he would express as much pleasure over it as a miser would be in discovering a bag of hid treasure. He was never better pleased with my employment, than when he had set me to prepare food or physic for the poor. He was hardly able to relish his dinner, if some sick neighbour had not a part of it; and sometimes, if any one of them was in want, I could not keep the linen

in his drawers.... Once a poor man, who feared God, being brought into great difficulties, he took down all the pewter from the kitchen shelves, saying, "This will help you; and I can do without it. A wooden trencher will serve me just as well."

The Life and Death of the Reverend John Fletcher, Works *11:346*

Time for Silent Reflection and Journaling

Blessing

"Happy are people who are hopeless, because the kingdom of heaven is theirs.

"Happy are people who grieve, because they will be made glad.

"Happy are people who are humble, because they will inherit the earth.

"Happy are people who are hungry and thirsty for righteousness, because they will be fed until they are full.

"Happy are people who show mercy, because they will receive mercy."

Matthew 5:3-7

Desiring to Do Good

My desire to do good is in response
to God's invitation to follow Jesus,
and it is in my control.
I can determine to extend hospitality
and goodness to all I meet.
I can decide to do good to all,
even to those who disagree with me
and turn against what I believe
is right and good.

Doing God's Justice

Prayer of Presence

Get up, LORD!
    Get your fist ready, God!
    Don't forget the ones who suffer!
Why do the wicked reject God?
    Why do they think to themselves
        that you won't find out?
But you do see!
    You do see troublemaking and grief,
    and you do something about it!
The helpless leave it all to you.
    You are the orphan's helper....

LORD, you listen to the desires of those who suffer.
    You steady their hearts;
you listen closely to them,
    to establish justice
        for the orphan and the oppressed,
    so that people of the land
        will never again be terrified.

                                    Psalm 10:12-14, 17-18

Scripture

> *My brothers and sisters, when you show favoritism you*
> *deny the faithfulness of our Lord Jesus Christ, who has been*
> *resurrected in glory. Imagine two people coming into your*
> *meeting. One has a gold ring and fine clothes, while the other*
> *is poor, dressed in filthy rags. Then suppose that you were to*
> *take special notice of the one wearing fine clothes, saying,*
> *"Here's an excellent place. Sit here." But to the poor person you*
> *say, "Stand over there"; or, "Here, sit at my feet." Wouldn't you*
> *have shown favoritism among yourselves and become evil-*
> *minded judges?*
>
> *My dear brothers and sisters, listen! Hasn't God chosen those*
> *who are poor by worldly standards to be rich in terms of faith?*
> *Hasn't God chosen the poor as heirs of the kingdom he has*
> *promised to those who love him? But you have dishonored the*
> *poor....*
>
> *My brothers and sisters, what good is it if people say they have*
> *faith but do nothing to show it? Claiming to have faith can't*
> *save anyone, can it? Imagine a brother or sister who is naked*
> *and never has enough food to eat. What if one of you said,*
> *"Go in peace! Stay warm! Have a nice meal!"? What good is*
> *it if you don't actually give them what their body needs? In*
> *the same way, faith is dead when it doesn't result in faithful*
> *activity.*
>
> *James 2:1-6a, 14-17*

First Wesley Reading

> I have a higher demand upon you who love as well as fear God. He whom you fear, whom you love, has qualified you for promoting his work in a more excellent way. Because you love God, you love your brother also: You love, not only your friends, but your enemies: not only the friends but even the enemies of God. You have "put on, as the elect of God, lowliness, gentleness, longsuffering." You have faith in God, and in Jesus Christ whom he hath sent: faith which overcometh the world: And hereby you conquer both evil and shame, and that "fear of man which bringeth a snare:" so that you can stand with boldness before them that despise you, and make no account of your labors. Qualified, then, as you are, and armed for the fight, will you be like the children of Ephraim, "who, being harnessed, and carrying bows, turned back in the day of battle?" Will you leave a few of your bretheren to stand alone, against all the hosts of aliens? O say not, "This is too heavy a cross: I have not courage or strength to bear it." True; not of yourself: But you that believe "can do all things through Christ strengthening you." "If thou canst believe, all things are possible to him that believeth."
>
> *Sermon 52, "The Reformation of Manners," Works 6:165*

Reflections

Many in our culture live out their lives in the fear that they will not have enough to provide for their needs to the end of life. And this fear is not entirely unfounded. There are many who do seem to miss out on the benefits of society, and who live and die with not quite enough of this world's goods. Perhaps there is reason to be concerned about how we are to live out our days, yet the scriptures suggest that being in want is not the greatest danger we face. There is something that is much more powerful and much more destructive than being in need, and that is having an abundance of this world's goods and believing they belong to us and not to God.

John Wesley was convinced that we should earn all that we can in an honorable way, and that we should save all that we can by reducing our own requirements. This was not so that his followers could store up riches, but rather so that they would have more to give to the poor and needy of the world....

We live in an age and culture where commitment to the poor seems to be waning and the desire for comfort and ease has dramatically increased, fueled by a constant bombardment of advertisers trying to convince us that useless luxuries are in fact necessities. Our culture teaches us that the accumulation of wealth is of much more value than helping those less fortunate than we are. For much of society, riches have taken the place of the Living God as our number one priority and love.

Is there hope for us in such a world? Can Christians live responsibly and faithfully in a world like ours?...How then should we live? By first offering all that we are, have, and hope to receive to God in complete commitment. This permits us to see all things, including the gift of life, as being placed in our hands by God for a purpose and for an accounting. An examen, or self-examination, at the end of every day is a good time to bring the activities and actions of the day before God for evaluation, blessing, or correction. It is this kind of personal self-examination that can lead us to faithful decisions about the investment of our lives and our resources in the enterprise of God in the world....

For Wesley, this meant dramatic commitment to the poor and needy and radical denial of his own desires for comfort and ease.

Second Wesley Reading

I walked up to Knowle, a mile from Bristol, to see the French prisoners. Above eleven hundred of them, we were informed, were confined in that little place without any thing to lie on but a little dirty straw, or any thing to cover them but a few foul thin rags, either by day or night, so that they died like rotten sheep. I was much affected and preached in the evening on, (Exodus xxiii.9) "Thou shalt not oppress a stranger; for ye know the heart of a stranger, seeing ye were strangers in the land of Egypt." Eighteen pounds were contributed immediately, which were made up four-and-twenty the next day. With this we bought linen and woolen cloth, which were made up into shirts, waistcoats, and breeches. Some dozen of stockings were added; all which were carefully distributed, where there was greatest want. Presently after, the Corporation of Bristol sent a large quantity of mattresses and blankets.

Journal from October 15, 1759, Works 2:516

Time for Silent Reflection and Journaling

Blessing

Do justice to your own soul; give it time and means to grow.... Take up your cross, and be a Christian altogether. Then will all the children of God rejoice.

Letter to John Trembath, Works 12:254

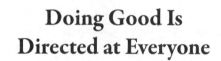

Doing Good Is
Directed at Everyone

Doing good is not limited
to those like me or those who like me.
Doing good is directed at everyone,
even those who do not fit my category
of "worthy" to receive any good that I
or others can direct their way.
This command is also universal in
that no one is exempt from it.

Tension Between Being and Doing

Prayer of Presence

*Loving God, lead me to find a healthy balance
   between being and doing.
Set me free from the bondage of unrealistic expectations
   and fill me with your enabling presence this very day.
I offer my prayer in the name of Jesus Christ
   whose life was a perfect balance of doing and being.* **Amen**.

Scripture

*While Jesus and his disciples were traveling, Jesus entered a
village where a woman named Martha welcomed him as a
guest. She had a sister named Mary, who sat at the Lord's
feet and listened to his message. By contrast, Martha was
preoccupied with getting everything ready for their meal. So
Martha came to him and said, "Lord, don't you care that my
sister has left me to prepare the table all by myself? Tell her to
help me."*

The Lord answered, "Martha, Martha, you are worried and distracted by many things. One thing is necessary. Mary has chosen the better part. It won't be taken away from her."

Luke 10:38-42

First Wesley Reading

All the commandments of God he accordingly keeps, and that with all his might. For his obedience is in proportion to his love, the source from whence it flows. And therefore, loving God with all his heart, he serves him with all his strength. He continually presents his soul and body a living sacrifice, holy, acceptable to God; entirely and without reserve devoting himself, all he has, and all he is, to his glory....

As he has time, he "does good unto all men;" unto neighbours and strangers, friends and enemies: And that in every possible kind; not only to their bodies, by "feeding the hungry, clothing the naked, visiting those that are sick or in prison;" but much more does he labour to do good to their souls, as of the ability which God giveth; to awaken those that sleep in death; to bring those who are awakened to the atoning blood, that, "being justified by faith, they may have peace with God;" and to provoke those who have peace with God to abound more in love and in good works. And he is willing to "spend and be spent herein," even "to be offered up on the sacrifice and service of their faith," so they may "all come unto the measure of the stature of the fulness of Christ."

The Character of a Methodist, Works *8:344-346*

Reflections

The tension between being and doing can be a pressure point of pain and anguish in a sensitive and sincere heart. We are often troubled and wonder why there never seems to be enough time or energy to pray *and* do. We struggle because compassion for others compels us to act while desire for intimacy with God compels us to flee into solitude.

To achieve a healthy balance here is to have discovered one of the keys of faithful and fruitful ministry. There is a strong temptation to deny the tension and, therefore, to fall into patterns of behavior that give attention to only one part of our formation. To recognize the invitation of Jesus to follow this one pathway that includes intimacy and action, prayer and compassion, can help save us from the destructive practice of paying attention to only part of our formation in Christ.

[For Wesley,] Methodist life was marked by a deep and authentic personal piety that led to a broad and uncompromising social involvement. Methodists were known for their prayers and their commitment to the poor and disenfranchised. This commitment resulted in persistent efforts to build houses of prayer and worship as well as consistent efforts to visit the prisons, build schools and hospitals, and work for laws which moved toward a just and peaceful social order....

In an age of unprecedented brokenness in the life of the individual and growing fractures in the human family, the practice of the Methodist way of Christian living holds great promise for a more faithful personal life and a more just and peaceful world.

We are created for companionship with God.... We learn the rhythms of spirituality through study, prayer and practice.... And we learn the rhythms of compassion and action through prayer, study and practice. Therefore, one of the effective ways of bringing healing to this tension or brokenness is to begin to practice a rhythm of life that includes paying attention to the journey inward as well as to the journey outward....

Love of God and love of neighbor are of a piece. They are two threads out of which we daily weave the seamless garment of spirituality.... Central to God's gracious activity of redemption in the world is the Christian's love of God and neighbor.

Second Wesley Reading

> Sometimes He acts on the wills and affection of men; withdrawing them from evil, inclining them to good, inspiring (breathing, as it were) good thoughts into them; So it has frequently been expressed, by an easy, natural metaphor, strictly analogous to *ruach*, *pneuma*, *spiritus*, and the words used in most modern tongues also, to denote the third person in the ever-blessed Trinity. But however it be expressed, it is certain all true faith, and the whole work of salvation, every good thought, word, and work, is altogether by the operation of the Spirit of God.
>
> *A Farther Appeal to Men of Reason and Religion,* Works *8:49*

Time for Silent Reflection and Journaling

Blessing

The LORD will protect you on your journeys—
whether going or coming—
from now until forever from now.

Psalm 121:8

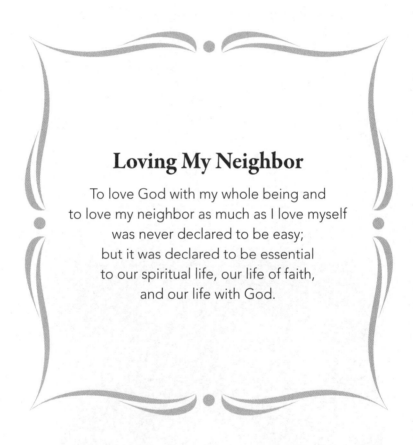

Loving My Neighbor

To love God with my whole being and
to love my neighbor as much as I love myself
was never declared to be easy;
but it was declared to be essential
to our spiritual life, our life of faith,
and our life with God.

Longing for More

Prayer of Presence

*Faithful Savior, who became one of us to make your way
and your Self known to humankind,
reveal your way and your Presence to me.
Help me lay aside the burdens and concerns of my life
long enough to hear your voice.
Lead me into the light of your truth
and prepare me for faithful and joyful discipleship.*
Amen.

Scripture

*Just like a deer that craves streams of water,
my whole being craves you, God.
My whole being thirsts for God, for the living God.
When will I come and see God's face?
My tears have been my food both day and night,
as people constantly questioned me,
"Where's your God now?"*

But I remember these things as I bare my soul:
  how I made my way to the mighty one's abode,
  to God's own house,
    with joyous shouts and thanksgiving songs—
    a huge crowd celebrating the festival!
Why, I ask myself, are you so depressed?
  Why are you so upset inside?
Hope in God!
  Because I will again give him thanks,
    my saving presence and my God.

Psalm 42:1-5

First Wesley Reading

And it is as impossible to satisfy such a soul, a soul that is athirst for God, the living God, with what the world accounts religion, as with what they account happiness. The religion of the world implies three things, (1) The doing no harm, the abstaining from outward sin; at least from such as is scandalous, as robbery, theft, common swearing, drunkenness: (2) The doing good, the relieving the poor; the being charitable, as it is called: (3) The using of the means of grace; at least the going to church and to the Lord's Supper. He in whom these three marks are found is termed by the world a religious man. But will this satisfy him who hungers after God? No: It is not food for his soul. He wants a religion of a nobler kind, a religion higher and deeper than this. He can no more feed on this poor, shallow, formal thing, than he can "fill his belly with the east wind.... All this is not what he longs for. This is only the outside of that religion, which he insatiably hungers after. The knowledge of God in Christ Jesus: "the life which hid with Christ in God:" the being joined unto the Lord in one spirit:" the having "fellowship with the Father and Son:" the "walking in the light as God is in the light:" the being "purified even as He is pure:"—this is the religion, the righteousness, he thirsts after.

Sermon 22, "Sermon on the Mount, Discourse 2," Works 5:268

Reflections

Our identity is found and formed by the God we worship and serve. Our life together as Christians is discovered, held together, and lived out based on our understanding of the God we have come to know and seek to follow.... We cannot escape the divisions, anger, hatred, and violence that are tearing apart the world that God so loved. Neither can we avoid the truth that so much of the anger, hatred, distrust, and division prevalent in the world has invaded the church.

In our honest moments, we know that this is not the way we want to live, should live, or are called to live by the God we have come to know through Jesus Christ. Thoughtful reflection brings the realization that the path we are on is not a path of fidelity or faithfulness to Jesus Christ. Rather, it is a path that leads us away from the very One we seek to follow....

I believe most of us do want to live a life of faithfulness and fidelity, I also believe that we are ready to once again get serious about our understanding of who God is, who we are, who we are together, and how we should live as creatures of the Creator God who has made all that is.

John Wesley was convinced that holiness is discovered in the practice of our faith in the practical and everyday routines of life. Therefore he fashioned for himself a way of living that included time for reading and reflecting upon scripture and other spiritual works and methods for putting into practice what he believed and what he heard God calling him to do.

Second Wesley Reading

> And now first it was that I had that full assurance of my own reconciliation to God, through Christ. For many years I had had the forgiveness of my sins, and a measure of the grace of God; but I had not till now that witness of his Spirit, which shuts out all doubt and fear. In all my trials I had always a confidence in Christ, who had done so great things for me. But it was a confidence mixed with fear: I was afraid I had not done enough. There was always something dark in my soul till now. But now the clear light shined; and I saw that what I had hitherto so constantly insisted on,—the *doing* so much and *feeling* so much, the long repentance and preparation for believing, the bitter sorrow for sin, and that deep contrition of heart which is found in some,—were by no means essential to justification. Yea, that wherever the free grace of God is rightly preached, a sinner in the full career of his sins will probably receive it, and be justified by it, before one who insists on such previous preparation.
>
> *Journal from August 10, 1738,* Works *1:128*

Time for Silent Reflection and Journaling

Blessing

By day the LORD commands his faithful love;
*   by night his song is with me—*
*   a prayer to the God of my life.*

Psalm 42:8

Concerning Holiness

His judgment concerning holiness is new.
He no longer judges it to be an outward thing:
To consist either in doing no harm,
in doing good, or in using the ordinances of God.
He sees it is the life of God in the soul;
the image of God fresh stamped on the heart;
an entire renewal of the mind in every temper and
thought, after the likeness of Him that created it.

Losing Our Way

Prayer of Presence

> I put all my hope in the LORD.
>> He leaned down to me;
>> he listened to my cry for help.
> He lifted me out of the pit of death,
>> out of the mud and filth,
>> and set my feet on solid rock.
>> He steadied my legs.
> He put a new song in my mouth,
>> a song of praise for our God.
> Many people will learn of this and be amazed;
>> they will trust the LORD.
>
> Psalm 40:1-3

Scripture

Simon Peter and another disciple followed Jesus. Because this
other disciple was known to the high priest, he went with Jesus
into the high priest's courtyard. However, Peter stood outside
near the gate. Then the other disciple (the one known to the
high priest) came out and spoke to the woman stationed at the

*gate, and she brought Peter in. The servant woman stationed
at the gate asked Peter, "Aren't you one of this man's disciples?"*

*"I'm not," he replied. The servants and the guards had made
a fire because it was cold. They were standing around it,
warming themselves. Peter joined them there, standing by the
fire and warming himself. . . .*

*Simon Peter was still standing with the guards, warming
himself. They asked, "Aren't you one of his disciples?"*

Peter denied it, saying, "I'm not."

*A servant of the high priest, a relative of the one whose ear
Peter had cut off, said to him, "Didn't I see you in the garden
with him?" Peter denied it again, and immediately a rooster
crowed.*

John 18:15-18, 25-26

First Wesley Reading

To quicken me in making a diligent and thankful use
of these peculiar advantages, I have the opportunity of
communicating weekly and of public prayer twice a day. It
would be easy to mention many more; as well as to show
many disadvantages, which one of greater courage and skill
than me, could scarce separate from the way of life you speak
of. But whatever others could do, I could not. I could not
stand my ground one month against intemperance in sleep,
self-indulgence in food, irregularity in study; against the
general lukewarmness in my affections, and remissness in my
actions; against a softness directly opposite to the character of

a good soldier of Jesus Christ. And then when my spirit was thus dissolved, I should be an easy prey to every temptation. Then might the cares of the world, and the desire of other things, roll back with a full tide upon me: And it would be no wonder, if while I preached to others, I myself should be a castaway.

Journal from March 28, 1739, Works *1:179*

Reflections

John Wesley was dismayed that those who professed to be Christians looked so much like those who made no profession of faith. He noted that the only observable difference was in opinions and modes of worship. But that is where the distinction ended. Radical and unqualified commitment to Christ was scarce, and therefore little observable fruit appeared in the life of the church. His emphasis on grace and holiness was an effort to change all of that. He believed that God would provide the necessary direction and power to live a distinctive life of holiness, if Christians utilized the means of grace that were available to all.

The fears that Wesley had for his time are shared by many in our time. It is not easy to find within any denomination in our time the essential core of scriptural Christianity that marked the primitive church. The "pure gold" of that primitive church has dimmed in our time as in Wesley's. We are often preoccupied with good but not essential things. It is not uncommon for the church in our time to have worthy goals, but no means to achieve them. Or, to have an honest desire to be faithful, but no carefully considered and taught way to access the means of grace that lead to faithfulness. And it is not uncommon for the church to be focused on itself and not on God as made known to us in Jesus Christ....

A life of personal and social holiness is as much a rarity in our time as in Wesley's. Now, as then, such a life will be misunderstood and will find opposition and mockery surrounding its practice. And yet, it is this determination to know God and be faithful to God that alone can lead to the fruit of scriptural Christianity. That fruit includes the comfort, assurance, fruitfulness, peace, and power promised to every faithful disciple. This is our inheritance as Christians....

An earnest commitment to walking with Christ always brings us to the road that leads to holiness, faithfulness, and God.

Second Wesley Reading

> While I was here, I talked largely with a pious woman, whom I could not well understand. I could not doubt of her being quite sincere, nay, and much devoted to God: But she had fallen among some well-meaning enthusiasts, who taught her so to attend to the inward voice, as to quit the society, the preaching, the Lord's Supper, and almost all outward means. I find no person harder to deal with than these. One knows not how to advise them. They must not act contrary to their conscience, though it be an erroneous one. And who can convince them that it is erroneous? None but the Almighty.
>
> *Journal from June 10-11, 1776,* Works *4:78*

Time for Silent Reflection and Journaling

Blessing

> *You teach me the way of life.*
> *In your presence is total celebration.*
> *Beautiful things are always in your right hand.*
>
> *Psalm 16:11*

Finding Peace with God

Prayer of Presence

Show us your faithful love, LORD!
Give us your salvation!

Let me hear what the LORD God says,
because he speaks peace to his people and to his faithful ones.
Don't let them return to foolish ways.
God's salvation is very close to those who honor him
so that his glory can live in our land.
Faithful love and truth have met;
righteousness and peace have kissed.
Truth springs up from the ground;
righteousness gazes down from heaven.
Yes, the LORD gives what is good,
and our land yields its produce.
Righteousness walks before God
making a road for his steps.

Psalm 85:7-13

Scripture

> "I have spoken these things to you while I am with you. The Companion, the Holy Spirit, whom the Father will send in my name, will teach you everything and will remind you of everything I told you.

> "Peace I leave with you. My peace I give you. I give to you not as the world gives. Don't be troubled or afraid. You have heard me tell you, 'I'm going away and returning to you.' If you loved me, you would be happy that I am going to the Father, because the Father is greater than me. I have told you before it happens so that when it happens you will believe. I won't say much more to you because this world's ruler is coming. He has nothing on me. Rather, he comes so that the world will know that I love the Father and do just as the Father has commanded me. Get up. We're leaving this place."

> *John 14:25-31*

First Wesley Reading

The general manner wherein it pleases God to set it up in the heart is this: A sinner, being drawn by the love of the Father, enlightened by the Son, ("the true light which lighteth every man that cometh into the world,") and convinced of sin by the Holy Ghost; through the preventing grace which is given him freely, cometh weary and heavy laden, and casteth all his sins upon Him that is "mighty to save." He receiveth from Him true, living faith. Being justified by faith, he hath peace with God: He rejoices in hope of the glory of God, and knows that sin hath no more dominion over him. And the love of God is shed abroad in his heart, producing all holiness of heart and of conversation.

Works Abridged from Various Authors, Works 14:212

Reflections

Our hearts race and we are nearly overcome with awe, wonder, and joy when we permit the words of Jesus to even get close to our center of awareness. "Those who love me will keep my word, and my Father will love them, and we will come to them and make our home with them" (John 14:23b). That God chooses to "live with us" is almost too much for us to comprehend. It takes getting used to. It requires a reordering of our ideas about God and about ourselves. Even as you read these words God is there with you to engage, reveal, guide, comfort, and companion. To remember this truth is to have our lives transformed. To forget it is to risk the danger and anxiety about today and tomorrow. To remember this truth is to face each day, no matter how difficult, or joyful, aware that God's loving and life-giving presence is with us always, and nothing can ever separate us from that presence.

It is this loving, steadfast, unshakable God who hovered over all creation and declared that it was very good (Genesis 1:31). This same God, revealed in Jesus, calls all to come home and intentionally dwell in God's presence. It is this God who chooses to move all that is toward justice, peace, harmony, and plenty—not just for a few, but for all. In Jesus we see a God who is moving all things toward the kingdom of righteousness, the kingdom of God. This is the God we see at work in creation and in the lives of the faithful. This is the God we desire, the God we long for, the God we want to follow in Jesus Christ.

Wesleyan theology encourages us to trust and obey an omnipotent God who is Lord over all. Fear, anxiety, and hopelessness are driven from our lives, for this sovereign God loves us and is able to care for us. We can live confidently and faithfully because God is able to care for and provide for all of creation.

Second Wesley Reading

> If, upon the closest search, you can find no sin of commission which causes the cloud upon your soul, inquire next if there be not some sin of omission which separates between God and you....Do you walk in all the ordinances of God? In public, family, private prayer? If not, if you habitually neglected any of these known duties, how can you expect that the light of his countenance should continue to shine upon you?...When you hear a voice behind you saying, "This is the way, walk thou in it," harden not your heart: be no more "disobedient to the heavenly calling." Till the sin, whether of omission or commission, be removed, all comfort is false and deceitful. It is only skinning the wound over, which still festers and rankles beneath. Look for no peace within, till you are at peace with God; which cannot be without "fruits meet for repentance."
>
> *Sermon 46, "The Wilderness State," Works 6:86*

Time for Silent Reflection and Journaling

Blessing

*Finally, brothers and sisters, . . . be in harmony with each
other, and live in peace—and the God of love and peace will
be with you.*

2 Corinthians 13:11

Being in Harmony with Jesus

I too will determine every day
that my life will always be invested
in the effort to bring
healing instead of hurt;
wholeness instead of division;
and harmony with the ways
of Jesus rather than
with the ways of the world.

Having the Mind of Christ

Prayer of Presence

Loving God,
I offer open hands, open mind, open heart,
    and a willing spirit
    to hear continually your calling and sending voice.
I abandon my life into your care
    with the assurance that you will lead me
    in paths of righteousness and goodness. **Amen.**

Scripture

Therefore, if there is any encouragement in Christ, any comfort
in love, any sharing in the Spirit, any sympathy, complete my
joy by thinking the same way, having the same love, being
united, and agreeing with each other. Don't do anything for
selfish purposes, but with humility think of others as better
than yourselves. Instead of each person watching out for their
own good, watch out for what is better for others. Adopt the
attitude that was in Christ Jesus:

Though he was in the form of God,
   he did not consider being equal with God something to
   exploit.
But he emptied himself
   by taking the form of a slave
   and by becoming like human beings.
When he found himself in the form of a human,
   he humbled himself by becoming obedient to the point
   of death,
   even death on a cross.
Therefore, God highly honored him
   and gave him a name above all names,
so that at the name of Jesus everyone
   in heaven, on earth, and under the earth might bow
   and every tongue confess
      that Jesus Christ is Lord, to the glory of God the Father.
                                          Philippians 2:1-11

First Wesley Reading

Whereas in that moment when we are justified freely by his grace, when we are accepted through the Beloved, we are born again, born from above, born of the Spirit. And there is a great change wrought in our souls when we are born of the Spirit, as was wrought in our bodies when we are born of a woman. There is, in that hour, a general change from inward sinfulness, to inward holiness. The love of the creature is changed to the love of the Creator; the love of the world into the love of God. Earthly desires, the desire of the flesh, the desire of the eyes, and the pride of life, are, in that instant, changed, by the mighty power of God, into heavenly desires. The whirlwind of our will is stopped in its mid career, and sinks down into the will of God. Pride and haughtiness subside into lowliness of heart; as do anger, with all turbulent and unruly passions, into calmness, meekness, and gentleness. In a word, the earthly, sensual, devilish mind, gives place to "the mind that was in Christ Jesus."

Sermon 83, "On Patience," Works 6:488

Reflections

When the disciples asked Jesus to teach them how to pray he taught them the prayer that has been our pattern of prayer ever since. In the Lord's Prayer, Jesus instructed them in prayer, but he did far more than teach the disciples to pray. He taught them how to live. In Luke's record Jesus reminds the disciples to stay focused, not on their need or on themselves, but on God. Our culture tells us in a thousand ways to stay focused on ourselves and outdo one another by caring for ourselves first. Jesus tells us that the best way to live fully and faithfully is to outdo one another in loving God and neighbor. To follow Jesus is to choose for ourselves the best way to live.

Living with Jesus is not easy. It never was. Even a casual reading of the Gospels shakes us up because they make it clear that living as a disciple brings earthshaking challenges. Jesus was physically with the first disciples to coach, teach, mentor, encourage, guide, protect, and provide. Still these early disciples were often perplexed, uncertain, and fearful. There were times when they just didn't get it.

The way Jesus plunged across boundaries and accepted everyone where they were was enough to keep them off balance as they tried to understand

and keep up with their leader. Of course, there were other times when they were filled with exuberance, confidence, courage, integrity, understanding, and strength. Those times when they rose to the challenge of living as a faithful disciple of Jesus....

Jesus still comes to us in the power and presence of the Holy Spirit to help us understand and to give us all the strength we need to prevail as faithful disciples.

Wesley believed that every person's life could be "hid with Christ in God, being joined to the Lord in one spirit." Such union with Christ required significant response from the believer and carried with it significant consequences. Life in Christ begins with deep faith in and an unqualified commitment to God. Our faith in and our practice of the ordinary spiritual disciplines, while worthy, is not enough. Our modest attempts to live a moral life fall far short of life in Christ. There is first this deep faith that Jesus Christ does love me, that he lived, died, and rose again for me, and today offers to me life abundant and eternal. It is such a faith that permits us to offer our lives to God without qualification.

Second Wesley Reading

> In a Christian believer *love* sits upon the throne which is erected in the inmost soul; namely, love of God and man, which fills the whole heart, and reigns without a rival. In a circle near the throne are all holy tempers:—longsuffering, gentleness, meekness, fidelity, temperance: and if any other were comprised in "the mind which was in Christ Jesus." In an exterior circle are all the *works of mercy,* whether to the souls or bodies of men....Next to these are those that are usually termed works of piety:—reading and hearing

the word, public, family, private prayer, receiving the Lord's Supper, fasting or abstinence. Lastly, that his followers may the more effectually provoke one another to love, holy tempers, and good works, our blessed Lord has united them together in one body, the Church.

Sermon 92, "On Zeal," Works 7:60

Time for Silent Reflection and Journaling

Blessing

Jesus said to them again, "Peace be with you. As the Father sent me, so I am sending you." Then he breathed on them and said, "Receive the Holy Spirit."

John 20:21-22

Living This Way

[The decision to live this way] will mean that
I will seek to heal the wounds of my sisters
and brothers, no matter if their social position,
economic condition, educational achievement,
or lifestyle is radically different from mine.

[The decision to live this way] will mean that
the words and acts that wound and divide
will be changed to words and acts that
heal and bring together.

[The decision to live this way] will mean that
movements that seek to divide
and conquer will become movements
that seek to unite and empower all.

[The decision to live this way] will mean that
the common good will be my first thought
and what is good for me will become
a secondary thought.

Only One Thing

Prayer of Presence

I am no longer my own, but thine.
Put me to what thou wilt, rank me with whom thou wilt.
Put me to doing, put me to suffering.
Let me be employed by thee or laid aside for thee,
exalted for thee or brought low by thee.
Let me be full, let me be empty.
Let me have all things, let me have nothing.
I freely and heartily yield all things
to thy pleasure and disposal.
And now, O glorious and blessed God,
Father, Son, and Holy Spirit,
thou art mine, and I am thine. So be it.
And the covenant which I have made on earth,
let it be ratified in heaven. **Amen.**
        A Covenant Prayer in the Wesleyan Tradition, UMH, 607

Scripture

When they finished eating, Jesus asked Simon Peter, "Simon
son of John, do you love me more than these?"

Simon replied, "Yes, Lord, you know I love you."

Jesus said to him, "Feed my lambs." Jesus asked a second time, "Simon son of John, do you love me?"

Simon replied, "Yes, Lord, you know I love you."

Jesus said to him, "Take care of my sheep." He asked a third time, "Simon son of John, do you love me?"

Peter was sad that Jesus asked him a third time, "Do you love me?" He replied, "Lord, you know everything; you know I love you."

Jesus said to him, "Feed my sheep. I assure you that when you were younger you tied your own belt and walked around wherever you wanted. When you grow old, you will stretch out your hands and another will tie your belt and lead you where you don't want to go." He said this to show the kind of death by which Peter would glorify God. After saying this, Jesus said to Peter, "Follow me."

John 21:15-19

First Wesley Reading

In 1727 I read Mr. Law's "Christian Perfection," and "Serious Call," and more explicitly resolved to be all devoted to God, in body, soul, and spirit. In 1730 I began to be homo unius libri; (1) to study (comparatively) no book but the Bible. I then saw, in a stronger light than ever before, that only one thing is needful, even faith that worketh by the love of God and man, all inward and outward holiness; and I groaned to love God with all my heart, and to serve him with all my strength.

Journal from May 14, 1765, Works 3:213

Reflections

It is so very simple and so very complete. We like to make it complex, hard to understand, and easy to avoid. But Jesus had a way of cutting through all the rules and their explanations to reveal the core truth of a faithful life. It was simple, challenging, and profound. His teaching was so clear it was hard to miss the point and so profound that it would take a lifetime of practice to fulfill its challenge. One day Jesus was confronted by some Pharisees about which commandment in the law was the greatest (Matthew 22:36). It could have been an honest question, or just another way to try to make Jesus appear irrelevant or wrong. And once again Jesus not only gives a clear and wise answer, but in doing so he gives a simple and complete blueprint for a life of faithfulness. Love God with all your being and love your neighbor as you love yourself.

There was a strong yearning for perfection deep within [Wesley's] life and he responded to that yearning by a disciplined life aimed at loving God and neighbor all day every day of his life. Such a disciplined life was not burdensome, but liberating. It was not a morbid affair under an unbearable burden of guilt going on to a destructive self-examination and condemnation. Going on to perfection was a way of living that offered freedom, meaning, and joy. To be moving toward perfection was to be moving toward life at its best.

The question Jesus asked of Peter in John 21:15ff, "Do you love me?" reveals a great deal about the essentials of our relationship with God. Three times Jesus asked, "Do you love me?" and three times Peter answered in the affirmative. Staying in love with God was the primary issue of a faithful life then, and it is today. For from such a life of love for God will flow the goodness and love of God to the world. It can be no other way. One who is deeply in love will be constantly formed and transformed by that relationship. And such a transformed life will be a natural channel of God's goodness, power, and presence in the world.

Second Wesley Reading

> What then is the perfection of which man is capable while he dwells in a corruptible body? It is the complying with that kind command, "My son, give me thy heart." It is the "loving his God with all his heart, and with all his soul and with all his mind." This is the sum of Christian perfection: It is all comprised in that one word, Love. The first branch of it is the love of God: And as he that loves God loves his brother also, it is inseparably connected with the second: "Thou shalt love thy neighbor as thyself:" Thou shalt love every man as thy own soul, as Christ loved us. "On these two commandments hang all the Law and the Prophets:" These contain the whole of Christian perfection.
>
> *Sermon 76, "On Perfection," Works 6:413*

Time for Silent Reflection and Journaling

Blessing

Dear friends, now we are God's children, and it hasn't yet appeared what we will be. We know that when he appears we will be like him because we'll see him as he is. And everyone who has this hope in him purifies himself even as he is pure.

1 John 3:2-3

Staying in Love with God

Staying in love with God is the
foundation to all of life.
It is in a vital relationship
with God that we are
enlivened, sustained, guided,
called, sent, formed, and transformed.

Guide to Each Day's Readings

Please see page 2 for a complete listing of abbreviations for original source books.

Day	Section	Original Source
1	Prayer of Presence	*TSQ*, 32
	Reflections	*WSR*, 43-44
2	Prayer of Presence	*Listen*, 55
	Reflections	*TSQ*, 19-22
	Blessing	*Listen*, 58
3	Reflections	*WSR*, 99; *Listen*, 12-13
4	Prayer of Presence	*Listen*, 23
	Reflections	*Listen*, 11,13; *WSR*, 15
	Blessing	*Listen*, 25
5	Prayer of Presence	*GTR*, 146
	Reflections	*TSQ* 64, 65; *WSR*, 141
6	Prayer of Presence	*Listen*, 37
	Reflections	*WSR*, 15
	Blessing	*Listen*, 40
7	Prayer of Presence	*TSR*, 75
	Reflections	*WYP* 3-4; *WSR*, 16
	Blessing	*Listen*, 106
8	Prayer of Presence	*TSQ*, 49
	Reflections	*WYP*, 149-150; *WSR*, 201
	Blessing	*WYP*, 72
	Boxed Content (Pg 42)	*TSR*, 21,22

Day	Section	Original Source
9	Prayer of Presence	*TSQ*, 69
	Reflections	*GTR*, 43-44; *WSR*, 194
	Blessing	*WYP*, 124
10	Reflections	*TSQ*, 40; *WSR*, 108
	Boxed Content (Pg 52)	Journal from April 1, 1762, *Works* 3:88
11	Reflections	*WSR*, 140-141
	Blessing	*WYP*, 146
12	Prayer of Presence	*WYP*, 72
	Reflections	*WYP*, 197-198
13	Prayer of Presence	*GTR*, 146
	Reflections	*TSQ*, 54-55; *WSR*, 201
14	Prayer of Presence	*Listen*, 90
	Reflections	*WSR*, 37
	Blessing	*WYP*, 92
	Boxed Content (Pg 70)	*TSR*, 37-38
15	Reflections	*WSR*, 99, 100
16	Prayer of Presence	*TSR*, 77
	Reflections	*WSR*, 91; *TSR*, 56, 61
17	Reflections	*WSR*, 108-109
18	Prayer of Presence	WYP, 84
	Reflections	*WSR*, 117
19	Reflections	*WSR*, 156
20	Prayer of Presence	*Listen*, 71
	Reflections	*WSR*, 185, 186
	Boxed Content (Pg 94)	*TSR*, 24

Day	Section	Original Source
21	Prayer of Presence	*GTR*, 40
	Reflections	*WSR*, 91, 92
	Blessing	*TSR*, 81
22	Prayer of Presence	*Listen*, 103
	Reflections	*WSR*, 124
23	Reflections	*WSR*, 171, 172
	Blessing	Adapted from *GTR*, 116
	Boxed Content (Pg 112)	*TSR*, 25
24	Reflections	*WSR*, 148
	Boxed Content (Pg 118)	*TSR*, 26
25	Reflections	*TSR*, 29-30, 32, 33, 34
26	Prayer of Presence	*GTR*, 60
	Reflections	*TSR*, 38-39
27	Prayer of Presence	*WYP*, 65
	Reflections	*TSR*, 55, 56, 65
28	Prayer of Presence	Adapted from *GTR*, 18
	Reflections	*WSR*, 207, 208
	Blessing	*WYP*, 84
29	Prayer of Presence	*GTR*, 18
	Reflections	*GTR*, 18-19, 21; *WSR*, 171
	Blessing	*GTR*, 24
30	Reflections	*WSR*, 83, 84
	Boxed Content (Pg 140)	*TSR*, 25-26

Day	Section	Original Source
39	Prayer of Presence	Adapted from *GTR*, 146
	Reflections	*WYP* 45-46, 49-50; *WSR* 36
	Boxed Content (Pg 194)	*TSR*, 42-43
40	Prayer of Presence	*UMH*, 607, A Covenant Prayer in the Wesleyan Tradition
	Reflections	*WYP*, 214; *WSR*, 207; *TSR*, 57-58
	Boxed Content (Pg 200)	*TSR*, 48

Photo by Mike De Bose

Rueben P. Job - 1928 – 2015

Bishop Rueben P. Job

Rueben Phillip Job was a United Methodist pastor and bishop, a best-selling author, and a leader in spiritual formation. His books include the best-selling Guide to Prayer series, *Three Simple Rules, When You Pray,* and many more.

Born on the family farm in Jamestown, North Dakota, in 1928, he loved the work of the farm and planned to continue the family farm until he received a clear call to ministry. He studied at Westmar College and later Garrett-Evangelical Theological Seminary. He married Beverly Ellerbeck, and together they raised four children: Deborah, Ann, Philip, and David.

He served as a pastor, a chaplain in the Air Force stationed in Europe, and later as World Publisher of The Upper Room. He was elected as a bishop of The United Methodist Church in 1984. In 2012, the Rueben P. Job Endowed Chair in Spiritual Formation was established at Garrett-Evangelical Theological Seminary in his honor.

A consistent thread to Rueben Job's writing centers on the call to live as a disciple of Jesus. From his commemorative book, *Life Stories* (Abingdon Press, 2010), he writes, "the call of God I sensed sixty-five years ago continues today....Some may sense a call to a specific task or vocation. However the highest calling anyone will ever receive comes first, "Follow Me". When we say yes to that call we offer ourselves to God as completely as we are able and God accepts and blesses the offering we make in remarkable ways. You who are reading these words have already heard, accepted, and responded to the highest call anyone can receive. The call to live as a disciple of Jesus.